Presented to

_____

On the occasion of

_____

From

_____

Date

_____

Mama's
Homemade Love

A Southern Woman Leaves a Legacy

Barbara Sims

PROMISE
PRESS

An Imprint of Barbour Publishing

Published by Promise Press, an imprint of Barbour Publishing, P.O. Box 719, Uhrichsville, OH 44683
http://www.barbourbooks.com

 Member of the
Evangelical Christian
Publishers Association

Printed in the United States of America.

Mama's
Homemade Love

DEDICATION

For Mama's grandsons and granddaughters-in-love,
Alan and Karen,
Mark and Debbi.
For her great-grandchildren,
Jessica,
Ethan, and Sarah,
To whom she left a rich legacy of love.

ACKNOWLEDGMENTS

A heartfelt "thank you" to each of you who inspired, edited, and encouraged: Angie, Bill and Elaine, Jim, Jack, Chester, Dr. Hilda Reynolds, and many others.

Also, to:

- Alan, for his permission to use the poem he wrote and read at Mama's funeral;

- Becky Freeman, who reminded me to "edit, rewrite, resubmit, but NEVAH give up";

- Margery, who has the blessed gift of forcing a manuscript to bleed red ink, encouraging the author, and satisfying the publisher with the same stroke of the pen;

- And to Don, who taught me to believe in myself, took me to new places, and inspired me to find my own frontiers.

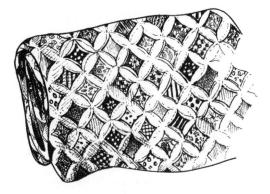

THE QUILT

By the time Mama was eighty-two years old, she still had not made a quilt. God had certainly blessed her with skillful hands: She could do almost any handwork she put her mind to. But she had yet to try her hand at this beloved craft. Then one ordinary Thursday in January, during Mama's weekly visit to her only daughter's house, she posed a simple question.

"Do you want me to make you a quilt?" Her voice was casual, as though this were a run-of-the-mill question.

Well, really, what daughter wouldn't want a quilt made by her mama? But Mama had more serious concerns. "If I die before it's done, will you finish the quilt? You have to promise me you will." I promised that I would finish the quilt.

Let me explain. I come from a long line of talented seamstresses who have left behind a legacy of fine handwork. Somehow, however, the sum of the Sciple's family talent was bestowed upon my cousin Elaine, the firstborn female of my generation. The gene for creating and stitching had definitely escaped the rest of us girls.

Oh, I did make my share of clothes for our struggling young family, but I lacked the legendary Sciple finesse. Once we had adequate funds for "store-bought" clothes, the sewing machine was put away, never to hum at our house again. Nevertheless, when Mama asked her question, I could promise to finish that quilt—because after all, Mama would never really die!

According to Mama, a quilt could be made two ways: handsewn or machine-stitched. That said, Mama made clear how she would proceed. "Quilts are supposed to be made by hand," she said firmly. "A real quilt is made by hand." While Mama's friends were busy making wedding ring, log cabin, and other popular quilts, she chose the cathedral window pattern for her own creation.

Before she began actually working on the quilt, Mama had to rummage around for all her scraps of material. Then every Thursday when she came to my house to visit and quilt, I would feel twinge after twinge of nostalgia. The tiny pieces of material were left over from things she had sewn, the clothes she had made for me as a teenager and her own "housedresses" that were her fashion trademark. She chose each scrap carefully, either because of the memories connected with it or because of its contribution to the color scheme. As news of Mama's latest project spread, many ladies in her small town donated little cotton pieces from their own scrap collections.

By early May, though, Mama had to put aside her handwork for a few days. As usual at this time of year, she was swept up into a flurry of baking, getting ready for one of her many visits to the beach with three of her sisters, all past their seventieth birthdays. But chest pains started as she mixed her famous cream cheese pound cake just one day prior to their scheduled departure. Via long distance telephone I directed her to unlock the front door and wait for the emergency help to arrive. The rescue unit took her to the hospital, and I hurried to join her there.

According to some of her relatives, Mama had been dying as long as they could remember, even before I was born. Her family teased her when her first child was born when she was thirty-six years of age; they told her she would never live to see her firstborn son graduate from high school. But she did, and she watched as her other two children received their diplomas as well. She was still there to see her grandchildren not only finish high school but also receive college and graduate degrees.

I never doubted that Mama was perpetual. She came from good genes. Her ancestors had lived to be past eighty at the time this country was settled. When I spoke of the possibility of Mama's death, it was always in terms of if, not when. Somehow I knew Mama was made out of better stuff than my generation. I was planning on her living for a long time.

Once I arrived at the hospital, I faced a sea of concerned faces and a flurry of activity. Mama was whisked away to the Coronary Care Unit and I was directed to the waiting area. Those first few hours made little sense; I remember a blur of faces—doctors, friends, and family. I remember the telephone ringing incessantly and the dense cigarette smoke fog that made my head pound.

Then, without warning, as dawn broke the next morning, my mind flashed back to that Thursday in January and the promise I had made. In the midst of my prayer I said out loud, "GOD, YOU KNOW I DON'T KNOW HOW TO MAKE A QUILT!"

Several days later my brother and I found the half-made cake Mama had been making. We disposed of the now-dried batter on the kitchen table. A neat stack of cathedral window squares was lying nearby, ready to take to the beach. Those carefully pressed pieces of fabric would be the first Mama used during the lengthy recuperation after her massive heart attack.

My quilt gave her always-busy hands something to do while her fragile body rested. The quilt gave each day a purpose and a goal, a reason to live. Mama wanted to finish that quilt before Christmas—and she did. On Christmas Eve she even wrapped it in holiday paper before bringing it to my house, as if it were a surprise to be opened with my other gifts.

She never discussed it with me, but I think she knew she had to recover. She knew I couldn't finish that quilt!

Mama did die, but not until years later. She never ever said "I love you" to her only daughter. But every time I look at my quilt, a labor of love, I know she did.

CORNBREAD

"When are we going to eat supper?"

Every day when we kids asked this question, Mama's answer was always the same: "When your daddy gets home and the bread gets done." At our house we never ate before Daddy got home and we always ate when the bread was done. Mama thought the difference between a good meal and a gourmet meal was the temperature of the cornbread!

And Mama knew the secret of making good cornbread—the cornmeal. After all, she came from a long line of Sciple millers who had once plied their trade in Germany. And besides, Mama didn't have to travel far for the real thing: She bought all her cornmeal from Sciple's Mill, Route One, Gholson, Mississippi.

George Ballentine Sciple was the proprietor of the mill when I was a youngster. George and Mama, born just a few weeks apart, were not only cousins, they were "buddies."

The mill, a wooden two-story structure, is next to Running Tiger Creek in Kemper County, Mississippi. My childhood memories are dotted with trips to the mill, where we kids used to fish in the creek. Water from that creek has turned the 3500-pound hand-hewn rocks for almost two hundred years, and those rocks are still turning today, grinding corn into meal almost as fine as flour. This meal is the best in Kemper County, and some say in the entire state of Mississippi. Mama thought it was the best in the whole world!

That area of the state was almost sacred to

Mama. She grew up there and walked through the woods to the one-room school with her cousin. His father, Chester, operated the mill. And my grandfather (Chester's brother), George Ellis Sciple, ran the general store just across the road.

When Mama and her older brother completed the education offered at the one-room school, the family moved to the nearby town of DeKalb. Later they migrated farther south and settled in Mobile, Alabama. But she never forgot Kemper County.

In a world where few things remain the same, Sciple's Mill has never changed. Mama said the place I visited when I was twelve was the same place she left when she was twelve. Back then everyone went to bed when it was "good dark," and they got up at daylight, and when I was a child we did the same. They had little need for electricity. To this day, I'm not sure anyone at Sciple's Mill has ever acknowledged daylight savings time. They don't need to, not when their lives follow the sun's age-old rhythm.

When we visited Kemper County, our entertainment was sitting on the front porch of the store each day and the darkened front porch of the house every night. Evening entertainment was simple. The kids all watched for lightning bugs as the grown-ups listened to the miller, Mama's grown-up cousin George, spin one of his many yarns. When an oil company leased land and drilled, we sat quietly and listened intently to the roar of the drilling rig. Other nights we could hear the sound of drums from a Choctaw campsite nearby. We would nod our heads and expect the Indians to arrive the next morning, bringing corn to be ground and hand-woven baskets for George to sell at the store. When Russia launched its first manned spaceship, everyone found a place on the front porch as soon as supper was over. We waited and watched until Sputnik crossed the sky.

Other times we spent the night with Mama's cousin Jesse Sciple and his family. They lived up the dirt road, a mile or so past the mill, in the house Mama had lived in as a youngster. The yards and the house remained just as Mama remembered them from her childhood. In the kitchen of this house Mama had learned from her mother how to make cornbread.

Even though Sciple's Mill was a special place to visit—one of life's pleasures to Mama—every trip was a mission. This was her opportunity to stock her cabinets with cornmeal. She carefully placed the thick brown bags, with "Sciple's Mill" printed on the front, in the trunk of our car for the ride home to Mobile.

Thanks to feature articles run by Memphis newspapers like *The Meridian Star, The Commercial Appeal,* and the *New Orleans Times Picayune,* the cornmeal from Sciple's Mill became famous. Word spread quickly, and the tourists came. Now, tourists have changed the face of the world, including the Holy Land, but they made no difference at

Sciple's Mill. Mama's cousin George remained his witty self. He still dressed in khaki pants and shirts that were always sprinkled with cornmeal. Customers still pumped their own gas and went inside to pay George's wife Ruby or her sister Eva.

If you are ever in the area, drop by. The mill will likely be open and a Sciple will be grinding corn. After seven generations, Sciple's Mill, Route One, Gholson, still produces the best stone-ground cornmeal. It had to be the best: Mama was never wrong when it came to cornbread.

It's nice to know that some things never change.

MAMA'S CORNBREAD
(in Mama's own words)

Shortening (a generous amount)
1 egg
Baking powder
Baking soda
Salt
Buttermilk
Cornmeal
Sugar (optional)

"Put a good bit of shortening in a black iron skillet and heat it in the pan 'til it gets real hot. Beat in an egg and a pretty good bit of baking powder until the mixture is fluffy. Add a pinch of baking soda and some salt and buttermilk and enough cornmeal to make it 'just thick enough.'

"Pour the mixture into the black iron skillet and bake the bread at 400 degrees for about twenty minutes, or until the edges get hard and the top is crusty brown. Serve the bread hot."

BISCUITS

My brother and I unpacked Mama's kitchen things last week. After careful consideration, we discarded a few. And then I saw the pan.

It was bent and browned from years of almost daily use. But in my heart I knew I could not throw away this oblong piece of tin. It contained too much of my past. This was Mama's biscuit pan. Her past was reflected in its sturdy tin shape.

There must have been something positive about being the second child in her family and the first female, but Mama could never think of one good thing. She was, however, always ready to talk about the disadvantages, and first on the list was learning to cook when she was a youngster.

"I learned to make biscuits before I could see over the top of the table," Mama often told me. "I stood on a stool, made the biscuits, and then Papa or Bud would put them in the oven." (Bud was her older brother and the stove was wood burning.)

When I was a child, that sounded pretty strange to me. Why would anyone so young have to learn to cook? Of course, I soon realized Mama's cooking was a necessity. Her family Bible records fourteen births, one every other year, except 1912, when two children were born, Ralph and Russell, Mama's twin brothers.

"Aunt Peggy would come every time a baby came as long as we lived at 'the old place,'" Mama remembered. "Aunt Peggy did the cooking when she was there. One time when I was about four or five years old, she pulled a chair, or maybe it was a stool, I can't remember, up to the kitchen table. I stood there beside her and she taught me to make biscuits."

So, with a little help from Papa and Bud, Mama was designated early to be the biscuit maker. Later she became the family cook whenever her mother Lillie was unable to cook (and, I suspect, when she was able and didn't feel like it).

Aunt Peggy's long-ago biscuit lessons paid dividends in the years to come. I doubt Daddy married Mama just because of her cooking skills, but I don't ever remember him backing his chair away from our family table when hot biscuits were served.

Mama was up every morning before the sun (without the help of an alarm clock), making biscuits for her family. If biscuits were baking, it was morning. If cornbread was in the oven, it was evening. Both were made daily and served hot.

During the era that my children call "the olden

days," biscuits were not sold in cans. When canned biscuits appeared on the grocery store shelves, Mama was not in the least impressed! "Who would ever put biscuits in a can and sell them? Biscuits are supposed to be homemade!"

During my teen years, however, I realized I could have about fifteen extra minutes of sleep each morning if I skipped breakfast. Mama was distraught—but not even those hot, flaky concoctions made from flour, buttermilk, and lard could entice me from my bed.

Yes, Mama used lard. Not Crisco, but plain, old-fashioned lard. At least, that's what Mama always called it. Our lard came packaged in an oblong waxed box and was purchased from the neighborhood grocery, "The Little Supermarket." (We called it "Mr. Kirk's," after Mr. Dewey Kirkpatrick, the proprietor.)

To make the biscuits, Mama stood at the white enamel-top table in the kitchen. She didn't use a mixing bowl; her biscuits were always mixed in a twelve-inch aluminum pan. The "real" biscuit pan sat nearby, its insides greased with lard.

During her entire almost-ninety years here on earth, Mama chose plain Gold Medal flour. "You can't make good biscuits with self-rising flour," she always said. Hers were good enough that I don't recall anyone questioning her choice of flour. Plain flour was the first ingredient put into the mixing pan, followed by salt, baking powder, and baking soda. She didn't own measuring spoons and she didn't need them. She just knew how much to use.

Mama would grab a hunk of lard and put it into the flour mixture, and then she mixed it with her hands. Next, she carefully poured in just enough thick buttermilk, mixing the dough all the while with her fingers. And her hands never even got sticky!

Mama had no need for a biscuit cutter. She simply pinched enough dough to make a small biscuit, rolled it between her palms, and then placed the dough in the greased biscuit pan. (In the South, one difference between city and country living was the size of biscuits. City biscuits generally were smaller.)

Once the biscuits were in the oven, before long an enticing aroma would fill the house. The biscuits smelled as good while they were baking as they tasted when they were done. Pretty soon everyone willing to get up early enough to eat arrived in the dinette for breakfast. (We were not yet acquainted with the word "dinette" so we called ours "the breakfast room.") When everyone was seated, Mama served up her light, fluffy, almost-perfect biscuits in the oblong pan. "Biscuits stay hot longer if you serve them in the pan," Mama reminded us often.

Mama always wanted her only daughter to learn to make good biscuits. Shortly after her death, I was more determined than ever to conquer what appeared to be such a simple task. I bought buttermilk and

Gold Medal plain flour—two absolute necessities, according to Mama—and I mixed the ingredients in a round pan. (I wondered if it might help if I stood on a stool when I mixed.) Unfortunately, the biscuits, the pan, and my hands were all a sticky mess!

Lately, I've been wondering if I should try again. Maybe the magic is in that bent, browned, oblong pan. Or maybe it's just the love.

MAMA'S BISCUITS

2 cups flour (Mama used Gold Medal)
4 teaspoons baking powder
1/2 teaspoon salt
1/4 teaspoon baking soda
1/2 cup shortening
1 cup buttermilk

Sift the flour and add the dry ingredients.

Cut in the shortening and add buttermilk, just enough so that dough mixes well. (If you want to be like Mama, mix with your hands.)

Take a pinch of dough and roll in your palms to make a small biscuit shape.

Continue until all dough has been used.

Place biscuits in greased oblong biscuit pan and bake at 450 degrees for 12–15 minutes.

Serve biscuits directly from pan. (Mama says they stay hotter longer that way.)

LUNCH

For Mama, the Great Depression did not begin with the fall of the stock market in 1929. Mama probably never heard the market when it crashed! She was twenty-eight years old and still living with her parents and seven of her thirteen siblings. Her salary provided support for the entire family.

The Sciple family—George, Lillie, and their children—had migrated south from Kemper County, Mississippi, to the greener grass of southern Alabama about 1917. The United States was in the middle of

World War I, and George hoped to make his fortune building government housing in the important seaport town of Mobile, Alabama.

A few short years later, long before he could make that fortune, the talented wood craftsman ended his work career. Family members said George had a bad heart. Others said George thought he had fathered enough children who could support him, so he didn't need to work.

Mama's oldest brother, Bud, left for Ohio to work in the rubber plants and never returned home. Two of the girls died when they were still babies. Three other girls, all younger than Mama, married; but Mama, though not lacking in beaus, remained single, lived at home, and supported the family.

Her sister Naomi still describes Mama as the "smartest one of all the children." Sadly, her education was interrupted when they moved to Mobile. To continue her schooling would have meant an eight-mile streetcar ride from Whistler to the high school, Barton Academy, in downtown Mobile. Mama's parents allowed their son to commute but not their oldest daughter.

Two years later, when the family moved downtown, Mama didn't reenter school. Instead, she found work at Kress, the five-and-dime store. Naomi says that Mama was "sort of in charge" of the lunch counter. I don't know what her job title was, but for most of her life, wherever Mama was, she was pretty much in charge!

Later she was hired by a locally owned department store, C. J. Gayfer and Company. Her old friends at Kress invited her to come back for lunch, but Mama always declined. She never had extra money to spend for lunches. After all, she was supporting a family of ten people. Still, Mama missed the social time her friends enjoyed on their lunch hour.

During the one hour she had for lunch, Mama would retrace the seventeen blocks she had walked to work earlier that day, hurrying home to eat a meal prepared by her mother. Then she would hike back to Gayfer's, arriving back on the sales floor before her hour was up. If you wonder how she could possibly walk so far, plus eat her lunch, in just one hour, that's because you didn't know Mama. Her brisk pace was one of her trademarks. In fact, she walked just as fast until she was past eighty years old.

Around this time, one of the earliest social service ministries in the city, a lunch ministry, started in a downtown Presbyterian church. The church opened its basement room, named it "The Carr Social Room" after an early minister, and invited the working girls to lunch. The ladies of the church welcomed them with cold tea in hot weather and hot tea when the seasons changed. Young ladies arrived daily, many of them carrying lunches bought at the lunch counter at Kress. Needless to say, Mama's lunches were always homemade.

Lunch for Mama was whatever remained from

the previous evening's meal. Her sandwiches were a leftover piece of chicken, or another meat, placed between two pieces of bread. Once in a while, she was lucky enough to tuck a teacake or other small baked confection inside her much-used Gayfer's paper lunch bag.

Anticipating the church social hour, Mama must have sped along even more lightly as she carried her lunch to work. She would have time to chat with her friends—Claudia, Katie, and Pauline—who also worked downtown. They likely exchanged stories about their current beaus.

One sunshiny day, someone had a Kodak and snapped pictures of the group as they sat in the side courtyard of the church. In Mama's old picture album, I can still see her smiling face surrounded by her friends. An ornate wrought-iron fence provides the backdrop for this moment in time.

If Mama's large family ate all the food from the night before, or if she didn't care for the leftovers,

Mama would leave for work the next day without a lunch, knowing she would have to walk home at noon regardless of the weather. Certain leftovers, like cornbread, biscuits, or baked sweet potatoes, reminded Mama of the one-room school in Mississippi. These foods meant you were "country" and "poor"; they were not fitting lunch fare for a young woman of the city.

Today the charming and historic Government Street Presbyterian Church still stands at the corner of Government and South Jackson in downtown Mobile. The same beautiful wrought-iron fence encloses the courtyard where Mama posed for pictures. And the lunchroom is still open.

But there have been changes. The church now serves food daily to the homeless, while downtown working girls eat lunch at upscale corner restaurants. Some days they spend more for lunch than Mama took home at the end of a week to feed the entire Sciple clan.

And the biscuit, which Mama was embarrassed to take to the lunchroom, is sold daily to rich and poor alike in certain fast-food restaurants within sight of the historic church. Perhaps, in our chaotic world, we are searching for something to cling to. . . something tangible from a bygone era.

FRUITCAKES

As I chopped and measured two quarts of pecans for the annual event of the Christmas season, I was transformed back in time to Mama's breakfast room table. There I was, not more than five years old, cutting up pecans for Mama's fruitcakes.

Making fruitcakes was an all-day affair for Mama, and some years the task spanned two days. (On those occasions, the pecans and fruit were cut one day, and the actual baking was done the following day.) Consequently, the day was carefully chosen. It couldn't be a Monday, as that was Mama's washday. And it couldn't be Mama's ironing day, either, for that was also an all-day task.

I always listened carefully as Mama discussed with herself which day she would bake the cakes. And as the day neared, anticipation filled my young mind, for I knew there would be bowls to scrape and spoons to lick. Every now and then a candied cherry might find its way to my mouth rather than the batter. I wouldn't have confessed to any personal guilt, but there was a strong possibility that I might find myself "too sick" for school the day the fruitcakes were to be baked.

When the day finally arrived, the breakfast room table was covered with all the makings and equipment. Mama had scrubbed and scalded the big white enamel dishpan with the red ring around the edge. It would serve as a gigantic mixing bowl.

There was the candied fruit, specifically two pounds each of cherries and pineapple, and small amounts of orange and lemon peel. "Not too much orange or lemon peel. It makes a cake taste bitter," Mama would say. "Citron makes a cake taste store-bought." I learned early that a taste like store-bought cake was not something to be desired or imitated.

Once she got started, Mama measured and creamed the sugar with the butter (real butter, of course). She used flour to "dredge" the fruit, and then later she added it to the cake batter. Only the freshest eggs were good enough, meaning those laid yesterday by our hens. Mama would put a big bottle of Watkins vanilla flavoring strategically on the table as a reminder to add flavoring to the batter.

A big bowl or pan held my carefully chopped pecans. At least the pan held most of the pecans. I was young, but old enough to know that forbidden fruit tastes sweetest.

Mama mixed the ingredients with loving care, assisted by a small but eager helper. A good fruit-cake mixture is sometimes too stiff to be mixed with a spoon, so we scrubbed our hands as vigorously as any surgeon. Then we mixed the batter carefully to make sure that the fruit and nuts were spread out evenly. I'm afraid, though, that my hands never reached Mama's standard of cleanliness until I was an adult—and even then I'm not sure they did.

Mama would always lay out an assortment of pans on the enamel-top table in the kitchen, two or three round pans for the "big" fruitcakes, several loaf pans, and one rectangular dish. These were called the "fruitcake pans." I never knew where she kept them; they just seemed to appear on this special day and vanish until the next holiday season.

The pans needed special preparation. First, brown grocery bags were used to cut liners for the bottom and sides of the pans. The paper had to be cut perfectly, Mama said, and she used the pans to draw her patterns. Then she cut wax paper and used it to cover the brown paper. With painstaking care, Mama made sure that each pan was smoothly lined.

Finally, the pans were filled with batter. Mama

decorated the cakes with the pecan halves, candied cherries, and pineapple that she had set aside earlier. I decorated my finger with batter from the mixing pan and spoons, savoring every bite of the sweet mixture.

The cakes all entered the oven at the same time and stayed there for unending hours. They filled the house with the first holiday aroma as they cooked for about one-and-one-half or two hours. (It seemed like at least five; for a young child it was an eternity!) When the cakes had finally baked to the perfect shade of brown that Mama expected, they were carefully removed from the hot oven and arranged on the table to cool.

Mama then made her yearly announcement: "Fruitcakes have to be cold before they can be cut." I knew what that meant. We would not cut the first fruitcake until Daddy was home and we were finished with supper.

Mama served the fruitcakes to friends, neighbors, and family, anyone who visited during the holidays.

Everyone always bragged on Mama's fruitcake as if it were a blue-ribbon cake. I have to admit, I felt a little proud when they paid their compliments. After all, I knew I had a major part in making the cakes: I cut the pecans.

I have carried on the family fruitcake tradition; I even baked them for Mama in her last years. She told me they were better than hers, but I never thought so. There was something about Mama's fruitcakes, a certain quality that set them apart from mine.

Maybe it's because I use a wooden spoon to stir the stiff batter. Maybe hers were better because they were truly "handmade." Or maybe there was just some secret that Mama knew, a secret that had to do with love and care and the willingness to take the time to do things right.

MAMA'S FRUITCAKE BATTER

1 pound butter
1 ½ pounds sugar
12 eggs
6 cups plain flour
1 cup wine, whiskey, or milk
     (Mama wrote in the margin
     of the recipe card,
          "I always use milk.")
Vanilla extract

Bake at 275 degrees for 1½–2 hours, or until lightly browned.

EASTER DRESSES

The year was 1945, and according to my way of thinking, two important things were happening in the world: World War II was raging and I was about to start school.

Mama started making clothes for me before I was born, even though she didn't own a sewing machine. She did her cutting and basting at home and went to her mother's house to do the "machine stitching."

When I was six, Mama decided it was time to

buy a sewing machine in preparation for the many school dresses I would need. By the time I completed graduate school, she had sewn many years' worth of school clothes.

I think *The Mobile Press* advertised the sewing machine. It was a name-brand Singer, a treadle machine in a cabinet, that rested on a wrought-iron frame. The Singer was a used model and cost five dollars. Late one afternoon Mama drove into the driveway in the dark blue 1939 Ford with the sewing machine perched on the backseat. I could hardly wait to get the machine inside so Mama could start sewing! I had visions of Mama sitting at that machine making lace and organdy dresses.

I don't remember Daddy being excited. "I don't know why you bought this big old used thing. How are you going to get it out of the car?" he asked Mama as he winked at me. As if he didn't know! Later, with a little effort, he carried the bulky object from the car and placed it near a window in the back room of the house, exactly where Mama told him to put it.

Mama stayed busy at the sewing machine, making solid, print, plaid, and striped school dresses. Each one was meticulously cut and basted before it ever reached the sewing machine. Then Mama pedaled away, making the old machine hum. The scene was repeated year after year as the dresses got bigger; meanwhile, the recipient got more particular about color, style, and fabric.

But the highlight of the year was always in the spring. Every year Mama turned out the prettiest Easter dress in the parade of girls at the West End Baptist Church in Mobile, Alabama. I just knew all the girls envied my Easter dresses!

For years Mama and I designed the dresses in downtown Mobile. We stood on the sidewalk outside the Vanity's show window while I chose the dress I wanted and Mama sketched a picture. When I got older, I made my own sketches from the pictures in my mind. I decided on the color and the fabric, never doubting Mama could, and would, make them. She always did. And they were exact replicas of the dresses I had envisioned.

The year I turned twelve I was all ready when Mama asked if I had decided what kind of Easter dress I wanted. Immediately, I sketched the dress on paper. I wanted my dress made from yellow pique and trimmed with eyelet. And I wanted black grosgrain ribbon tied into bows at the neck and on each pocket.

Mama bought yellow waffled pique, white eyelet, and black ribbon. She pieced together several patterns, and then cut and lovingly basted the dress. I tried on the basted bodice while Mama held the skirt in place. I thought I was a princess—and Mama was surely a fairy godmother with magic in her sewing fingers.

Easter morning finally arrived. With my black

patent leather shoes to match the black ribbon, and new socks trimmed with eyelet lace to match my dress, I was sure I was the envy of every girl at church. I loved my dress so much, I even wore it back to church that night.

But my pride was soon shattered. Each of my four years in the junior department at West End Baptist Church, I took part in the "Junior Memory Drill," what was commonly called the "Bible Drill." Every year I advanced to the district drill to represent our county. And every year I wore my Easter dress because it was my best dress.

The year of the yellow pique dress, the district drill was held in Jackson, Alabama. Two memorable things happened on my trip to Jackson: I placed first in the competition and received a scholarship for a week at our state camp, where I would compete for the state title; that was the first thing. The second thing was that I was made aware by one of my friends that I was the only one in "our group" who wore homemade clothes. Everyone else bought their clothes, mostly downtown at Gayfer's, still Mobile's leading department store.

Homemade sounded like a dirty word. As I looked at what I thought was my most beautiful dress, I struggled unsuccessfully to hold back my tears. In that instant I decided I would never wear another homemade dress. Humiliated, I was certain that every dress I had thought beautiful must have actually been tacky. I was probably branded for life for having worn them. I would never wear another homemade dress, or any other homemade garment, as long as I lived.

Of course when I started to dress the next day, I realized I had a serious problem. I did not own any clothing that was not homemade by Mama, not even a pair of shorts. Mama stood beside my bed as I sat and cried, dressed in my homemade pajamas. She persuaded me to dress. She didn't waste her breath talking about the sewing machine or how much she loved to sew for me. She didn't even mention that I could have more clothes because she made them or that I had the opportunity to choose colors.

No, all Mama said was one simple sentence: "Get up, find something to wear, and get dressed." I knew I was destined to wear the ugly-word dresses for eternity, while everyone else in "the group" enjoyed real, store-bought clothes, clothes that had labels sewn at the neck.

For the next few years I pleaded and pouted to no avail. I designed the clothes in my mind, Mama made them on the machine, and I wore them. But I didn't feel like a princess, and I was certain Mama was not a fairy godmother!

Finally, I approached the problem from another angle: I asked for a bought dress for Christmas. Mama was skeptical, but by this time I was old enough that she gave me her car keys, sent me to Gayfer's, and told me to find the dress I wanted. She was about to teach me the lesson that today we call natural consequences.

My heart racing, I took a friend with me—and a mental image of the beautiful store-bought dress I would purchase. It would be a beautiful shade of blue, trimmed in heavy blue lace, the same shade as the dress that would fit me perfectly. It would have a dropped waist, the newest style of the season. I could hardly wait to see it.

But when we reached the store, the dress eluded me. Instead, I returned home with a dress with no lace, a dropped waist that did not drop far enough on my tall body, and a too-short skirt. But the worst part was the color. The dress was dark brown. The dress was acceptable to me only because it was store-bought.

Even so, I wore my dress proudly the Sunday before Christmas—but no one noticed. No one complimented my dress or noticed that it had a label at the neck. Reality set in as I looked in the mirror.

This dress was not pretty, and it didn't fit well. This time I cried because my dress was store-bought, and I hated it! But Mama insisted that I wear the dress, not only to church every Sunday but to every other special occasion.

Long before the first signs of spring, I knew I wanted a homemade Easter dress. Now I recognized a superior piece of clothing. The best dresses were handmade, especially if the hands were Mama's.

I bought a copy of *Seventeen* the day the spring clothing issue arrived at the drugstore. I picked out the prettiest dress, a pink-and-white-checked gingham "Johnathan Logan" trimmed with white organdy and black velveteen ribbon. I showed the picture to Mama, who was glad to be back in the dress construction business for her only daughter. She bought the fabric and pieced her old patterns together again. My Easter dress that year was the prettiest dress I had ever owned!

Sunday morning brought oohs and aahs from all my friends and many of the grown-ups. I was certain the dress Johnathan made was not nearly as pretty as Mama's garment. I imagined, just for a moment, that I looked a little like the model in *Seventeen*.

The pink-and-white-checked dress was the last Easter dress Mama made on the old Singer. Portable electric machines were on the market now, and Mama joined all the other sewing women of America as they traveled down the road of modern convenience. Mama sold the old Singer to a friend for twenty-five dollars.

Easter is still my favorite Sunday of the year, even though I no longer care whether I have something new to wear. But I love to watch families as they enter the church sanctuary dressed in their Easter best. Many of the children's little dresses come from specialty shops; they clearly strive for that certain "homemade" look.

Mama was just about fifty years ahead of her time. Funny how that works. I suspect she knew all along that the best clothes are those handsewn with love.

GUMBO

I was born a few miles from beautiful Mobile Bay. I thought everyone grew up near the water, everyone knew how to swim, and all gumbo tasted like Mama's.

"Get your bathing suits on. We're going to Alba Beach." We were always glad to hear this familiar command on hot summer afternoons. Alba Beach was a simple stretch of sand on the western shore of the bay. A narrow, aging pier jutted over the water from the sandy shoreline, and at high tide the water near the pier was deep enough for swimming.

This excursion had a twofold purpose. Yes, it provided hours of delight for us children on a steamy summer afternoon, but Alba Beach was also a place for Mama to crab. And for Mama, crabbing was the first step in making gumbo. Mama loved to scoop those shellfish from Mobile Bay.

She always came prepared. In our freezer we kept a plastic bag filled with chicken necks and backs and other undesirable pieces of meat. Mama would take the meat from the freezer in time to thaw for crab bait. Besides the bait, Mama only needed a ball of heavy string, her long-handled crab net, and a tub for the crabs she knew she would catch. All these items were piled into the car, along with three or four happy children clad only in bathing suits. Mama always wore her housedress and a sun hat.

When we arrived bayside, two of us children would grab the handles of the aluminum washtub filled with crabbing apparatus and carry it to the wide area at the end of the pier. Mama cut string into ten- to twelve-foot lengths, attached bait to one end of each length, and tied the other ends securely to the pier posts. She put out about eight or ten lines all together, and then she waited for the crabs to come to dinner.

Exciting things happened beneath the water. Even Mama, despite her ability to see almost everything her children did, could not see the big blue crabs as they gathered and attached themselves to the meat. But when they tried to move their meal to deeper and safer waters, Mama would gently tug on the string.

"Don't pull too hard or too fast," Mama would remind us when we were learning to crab. "You'll scare the crab and he'll let go." It was an art, pulling the string with the meat and crab attached off the sandy bottom and scooping them into the net. Sometimes it worked and sometimes it didn't. For

Mama, a champion crab catcher, most of the time it worked. She quickly dumped the live crab into the waiting tub and covered it with a damp burlap sack.

Mama wanted two to three dozen crabs, enough for a big pot of homemade gumbo, but she was delighted when she caught more. In those days, crabs were big and they were plentiful. They were, and still are, filled with the most succulent meat that comes from beneath the water.

My first encounter with those crabs would likely be at lunch the next day in an omelet. I was an adult before I realized the hours of work between crab net and omelet pan. But I always knew the real reason why God created crabs: so that Mama could make gumbo.

Mama's gumbo was like many of her other dishes —extraordinary! That's because, as usual, her gumbo was different. It had to be. She caught the crabs. She grew the tomatoes and picked, peeled, and mashed them. She also planted the okra and cut it while it was still young and tender. The green peppers and onions came from her garden, too. "Everything needs to be fresh to make good gumbo," Mama would say as she browned the flour for the roux.

Mama made a perfect brown roux long before Cajun cooking became popular. To make this mystical, almost-burnt flour mixture, the basis for her gumbo, she melted a generous amount of shortening in the "deep black skillet." Daddy had given her this essential utensil in 1931, the year they were married. When the temperature of the grease met with her approval, she added flour. Mama patiently stirred as the mixture turned from blond, to brown, to almost burnt. Then she carefully dumped the muddy mixture into boiling water in her big aluminum pot.

One by one, she added all the other ingredients at their appointed times while the mixture simmered under her watchful eye. By suppertime, she had created another big pot of the best gumbo imaginable.

She served that gumbo to family, immediate and extended. She delivered it to the sick and "old." She served it with green salad, crackers, and dessert to visiting preachers, and regular ones, too. Mama's own pastor once said, "I think heaven is going to be a washtub of Mrs. Whatley's gumbo and me, the only person hungry!"

One day the inevitable occurred: I told Mama I wanted to learn to make gumbo—and I wanted her recipe. Her reply came quickly. "I don't have any recipe for gumbo! You just have to make the roux and put the other things in it." After several disastrous attempts, eventually I did improve, although Mama never did approve (and probably for good reason). No wonder it's never matched Mama's, though: I don't grow my own tomatoes, I buy frozen okra, I brown my roux in the microwave, and I buy seafood at the grocery store!

Not long after my sons married, I received a call from each of the daughters-in-love. They wanted to learn to make gumbo for their husbands. Like Mama, my reply came quickly: "I don't have a recipe!"

But then I did the same thing Mama did. I taught them step by step. That's the best way to learn to cook. And it's the best way to learn any of life's important lessons, especially when taught by a mother to her children.

MAMA'S GUMBO
(in her own words)

Fresh-picked crabmeat or shrimp
Shortening
Flour
Water
Fresh, ripe tomatoes
Onion
Celery
Green bell pepper
Butter
Salt and pepper
Okra

"It is better to have fresh-picked crabmeat that is less than twenty-four hours from Mobile Bay. If this is not possible, you can use fresh shrimp, if you buy them from someone you know and trust who has a shrimp boat. Then you will know they are fresh.

"To make the roux, you put a pretty good bit of shortening, or oil (but it won't brown as good), in a deep black skillet. Then get the skillet and the oil hot, but not too hot because it will burn. Add the flour—plain flour. The amount of flour depends on how much shortening you have used. You will know when you have enough. This needs to be thick.

"It takes a long time to make the roux. You need to stand at the stove and stir until the flour is the color you want it to be. If you leave the stove, it probably will burn. It needs to be a little darker than mud. If it is any lighter, the gumbo will be pale. If it is much darker, the gumbo will taste burnt.

"While you are stirring the roux, put some water on in your biggest aluminum pot. It should be about one-fourth full. The water needs to be boiling before the roux gets to the right color. Then carefully pour the roux into the boiling water. If you aren't careful, you may get burned.

"Add real ripe fresh tomatoes from your garden

that have been mashed up. If you don't have a garden, you will have to buy canned ones, but they won't be as good.

"Cut up the onion, celery, and bell pepper. Sauté and put them into the boiling mixture. Then put the seasoning in and let it simmer.

"You know you need to put salt and pepper in it.

"If you have just boiled a chicken for chicken salad, don't throw away the broth. You can put it in the gumbo now. Put the okra and the seafood in last. You don't want to cook them too long. As soon as the okra is done, the gumbo is ready. But let it cool and put it in the refrigerator. It will be better tomorrow. Be sure to cook some rice.

"Invite the preacher."

FLOWERS

The first time Mama's flowers made *The Mobile Press* was in 1955. The newspaper listing read:

> House for sale. Bellingrath Gardens of Mertz Station. Numerous trees and beds filled with flowers at their peak. Come and see. 613 Shannon Avenue.

The description was accurate. Mama was a

flower lover, and for sixteen years she had worked to make 613 Shannon Avenue a showplace. Hydrangeas lined the driveway, reaching past the lower level of the windows. Mama enjoyed their beautiful shades of blue from the kitchen windows—the place she seemed to spend most of her waking hours, her hands in the kitchen sink.

Flowers grew along the front of the house. Another flower bed separated the front yard from the back, then turned and followed the fence line to the street. The beds were outlined with bricks and filled with bridal wreath and pink "Pride of Mobile" azaleas. Thick bunches of thrift made a colorful boundary within the brick border. Mama added bedding plants each spring to complete the array of color.

When we children were bored on hot summer afternoons, we picked berries from the chinaberry tree in the side yard and fought chinaberry battles. The tree also gave Mama another reason for a flower bed; she worked diligently and built a bed about six feet in diameter encircling the small tree trunk. We called it the coleus and caladium bed. When she planted them, the coleus were tiny stems and the caladium were merely bulbs. By the end of summer, touched by Mama's hand and water from frequent afternoon showers (or a bucket when necessary), the coleus and caladium bed flourished. Every neighbor who came to visit stopped to look.

Even though Daddy was a man who loved the soil, he did not share Mama's love of flowers. "I don't plant anything I can't eat," Daddy would say if she asked him to help her weed the beds. Mama would then ask for help from her equally unenthusiastic children, who, unlike their father, did not have the rank to refuse. Mama made sure her flower beds were the best in town.

Yes, the description in the newspaper was accurate. The odd thing was that the home was for sale.

Daddy built that house for Mama the year I was born, 1939. She had not wanted a new house; she'd been happy living on Margaret Street near downtown Mobile, and she was certain her beautiful hardwood floors would buckle from the "buckets of tears" cascading down her cheeks as she packed to move. Mama had only agreed to move to Shannon Avenue when Daddy promised her he would never ask her to move again. And he didn't.

Sixteen years later, Mama and her three children made the decision to leave Shannon. Each of us knew Daddy wanted to move again, back to the area of his birth, back to the country. Even so, Mama hated to leave her beautifully landscaped yard for a five-acre homesite that had been recently plowed with a tractor. But the house on Shannon sold, and with it went sixteen years of flowers lovingly tended by Mama's gloved hands.

The house in the country was larger and nicer. Daddy cut the white virgin oak from his land and sent it to the sawmill, where he handpicked each board for the hardwood floors. He wanted Mama to be happy in the new house. And she was happy with the house—but not with the yard.

The bare, grassless dirt would never do. The sandy soil was completely dry a few hours after a heavy rain, and there were no flowers. So with a few plants and cuttings from Mobile, her old garden tools, and her love of dirt and flowers, Mama got busy!

She made flower beds and planted azaleas, alternating them with bridal wreath. She made a new circular bed and filled it with hot-pink prickly thrift. A purple wisteria climbed an oak tree near the front entrance, welcoming guests with fragrance and beauty. Mama worked hard and turned her new yard into another "charm spot."

Even though Daddy died seven short years later, Mama never regretted the move. She lived in that house, surrounded by her flowers, her remaining twenty-seven years.

This year, the homeplace sold. When I pass the

vacant house during the week, I always slow down. It seems like the reverent thing to do.

I was overwhelmed this spring with the wild beauty, which remains four years after Mama's death. The azaleas have grown past the tops of the windows on the front of the house. No foliage is visible, only a profusion of pink that looks as if someone poured a gigantic bucket of pink paint over the plants.

In a recent issue of *The Mobile Press* I read this by Jay Grelen, a local columnist, who happened to be in Mama's old neighborhood:

> I didn't stop to measure but some of the [azalea] bushes seemed to grow six or eight feet tall. They were so thick with blooms, that from the road, you couldn't see any green, as if someone had pink blankets on the bushes to protect them from a late frost.

Surely he must have passed by Mama's house. Mama knew how to coax beauty out of the bare earth—and that beauty is still flowering, years after Mama's death.

FIG PRESERVES

When Daddy moved the family to Shannon Avenue from downtown Mobile, he agreed to move the fig trees as well as the furniture. In fact, after he sold the house Mama didn't want to sell, Daddy agreed to almost everything Mama wanted!

But there was one problem. Daddy planted the fig trees in the wrong place.

The white frame house with brick columns on the front was built on a one-acre lot. In front of the house was a big yard, and behind the house was a huge two-story, double-car garage. The front yard seemed huge to me as a child, but when I drove by recently to take some pictures, the house appeared to have gravitated toward the street, making the front yard appear much smaller. The house and the garage looked like miniature versions of where I once lived. But a person can still stand in the street (it used to be dirt, but now it's paved), look to the left of the house, and see the two-story garage at the end of the driveway.

Daddy planted the fig trees behind that garage. I grew up hearing the story of how Mama was sure she would never make fig preserves again. "My fig trees will never bear fruit there," she lamented. She was certain the trees were not happy where they had been planted.

Mama thought her fig trees should have been planted beside the back door. "A fig tree won't live if it can't hear the dishes rattle in the dishpan," Mama said. "And it needs to be close enough to the house so it can be watered with the dishwater." She told Daddy he'd be sorry he planted those fig trees in the wrong place. After all, he would never taste her homemade fig preserves again.

But something strange happened over the years.

On warm summer nights the kitchen windows were left open for the cool breezes. The fig trees must have listened carefully and heard a certain rattling in the sink as Mama washed the supper dishes. And I suspect she made many trips out the back door, carrying dishwater to pour gently around the roots of her trees.

Not only did the trees live, they actually flourished.

For several years Mama worried they would die. When they didn't, she needed something new to worry about. So she began to worry that they would grow too tall.

Her worrying never stunted their growth. The fig trees grew so tall that Mama had to climb a stepladder to pick her figs. Eventually the ladder wasn't tall enough, and she fretted as the succulent fruit spoiled in front of her eyes, beyond her reach.

But Mama was well known for rising to meet any occasion. So she enlisted three or more of us children, however many of us resided at 613 Shannon at the time, in the "fig-picking brigade." She sent this elite corps up the stairs and out the second-story window, onto the sloping roof of the garage. There, little hands could easily reach the figs and place them in an aluminum pan. Then we brought the figs back through the window into the second story of the garage, down the stairs, and placed them safely into Mama's waiting hands.

Mama was not only happy that the figs were picked, she was happy when the children had their feet safely back on the ground. She cautioned us repeatedly, "Don't get too close to the edge. Just pick the figs you can reach without leaning out too far. And don't ever go on the roof to play!"

While Mama was inside washing the figs,

removing any that might have been pecked by birds, those of us in the brigade were outside deciding whether we dared go on the roof to play. By the time she had the figs covered with sugar and cooking over a slow heat, we had made our decision. We were experiencing the sheer joy of playing in forbidden territory—the cool shingles of a sloping roof on a hot summer day.

I spent many happy hours on that small space that seemed like it was almost as high as heaven. Sometimes I played with the other fig-pickers, or I had secret club meetings with my neighborhood girlfriends. But more often I climbed out the window with a book, which, like a magic carpet, took me anywhere I wanted to go.

While Mama cooked her figs, I read all about the Bobbsey Twins, Nancy Drew, and the Hardy Boys. I read about faraway countries with cathedrals, castles, and gardens, and I dreamed of someday going there.

Mama never missed me. She was busy adding

thin lemon slices to her figs as they cooked over the low heat. "Lemons make the figs taste tart and not so sweet. It makes them better." And she was busy getting the jars ready. They had to be washed and scalded. Then she turned them upside down to drain and cool on a clean dishtowel on the enamel-top table. When she was finally done, she carefully spooned the homemade preserves into the jars, sealed, and stored them until we ate them for breakfast.

One summer Mama made so many pints and quarts of fig preserves that the kitchen cabinets overflowed. Daddy built special shelves downstairs in the garage to store the figs, other preserved fruit, and canned vegetables.

But Mama never knew I spent most of many summers on that rooftop. When she would call "Barbaraaaaaaaa Jeannnnnnn!" (in the South, two-word names are the rule), I'd scramble down from the roof like my life depended on it. I'd fly into the garage, down the stairs, across the backyard, and through the back door, just as she finished the last "en" of Jean. (She always thought I was upstairs in the garage playing, which was allowed.)

To this day, when I remember fig preserves, I still feel the thrill of those forbidden visits to my secret playground. In my high space on the garage roof, I peeked into worlds of wonder, while the sweet smell of cooking figs floated through the air. And meanwhile, the fig trees listened to the distant rattle of dishes and just grew taller and taller.

HOUSECLEANING

With three or more children in residence for twenty-five years, Mama's house was often cluttered. Cluttered, yes, but never dirty. Mama had a master plan that included major cleaning twice each year, a routine she had learned from her mother.

On the first warm sunshiny day of spring, Mama began spring cleaning in her mind. Several weeks might go by before the actual work started, but the first step was to find a week on the calendar when Mama did not have any commitments. Once the week was chosen, Mama armed herself with Clorox, Dutch Cleanser, ammonia, and furniture and floor polish. Then she enlisted the help of her children, who were sometimes willing and sometimes not. When the chosen week arrived, she worked to rid the residence of dirt, grime, and germs. When she was finished and everything sterilized, major surgery could have been performed in any room with little danger of infection. (If cleanliness is next to godliness, Mama was probably renamed "Saint Helen" when she got to heaven.)

The same ritual occurred each fall, except then it had a different name. On the first cool, crisp morning, Mama began the fall cleaning dialogue in her mind—setting the date for another major recleaning of her not-so-dirty house.

"Real" housecleaning was a room-by-room adventure for Mama. She always started in the living room and dining room, which were separated by an archway. When Mama cleaned, she began at the top and worked down, cleaning the floors last. So it made sense that the chandeliers were cleaned before anything else. "You need to clean the light fixtures first," Mama said. "If you wait until later to clean them, their dust will get on something you have already cleaned." I didn't understand much about how dust traveled, but back then everything she said was gospel.

From the light fixtures, Mama moved to the crown molding. She climbed up and down, up and down, moving the ladder as she worked her way around the tall ceilings of the two rooms.

By this point, little was left in the room to inhibit her; she had removed all washable accessories to the kitchen to be cleaned. One by one, she took the framed pictures from the walls, carefully dusted them, and stacked them face down on the cushionless couch bottom. She placed the couch cushions and other small pillows outside in a "safe place" where they could "sun." With painstaking care, she washed and starched curtains, then washed the windows inside and out, using vinegar water, I think. We didn't know about Windex back then. It may have been available, but Mama did things the thrifty way, which was usually the hardest way.

When she had cleaned everything in the room that could be cleaned with liquid, all the rest was vacuumed and revacuumed. The hardwood floors were always Mama's pride and joy wherever she lived, and she waxed and buffed them until they shone. If Mama had been in the military, she surely would have been the "Company Commander in Charge of Inspection." She moved from room to room, dismantling and recreating the room to meet her standard of cleanliness. Not a closet or drawer, nook or cranny were left untouched during house-cleaning week. Mama gauged the level of cleanliness of her house by the smell inside. It only met her standard of cleanliness when she could say, "This house smells as fresh as sunshine!"

I was always most intrigued when I helped clean

what we call today the master bedroom. Here in "Mama and Daddy's room" I found drawers to open and treasures to touch, all of which were off-limits to little hands the remaining fifty weeks of the year. But some tasks in this special room were a little perplexing. Once when I thought we were through, I learned we had yet another task to complete.

Mama kept an old pillowcase on a shelf in her closet, which she called "the ragbag." In it she stored old towels and flannel pajamas that could likely experience a second career as a dust cloth or a cleaning rag. On one particular day I sat beside Mama as she cleaned out the rag bag. First, she dumped all the folded pieces of fabric on her bed. Then she opened each one and chose a few to use for the "new" cleaning rags. We refolded the others and returned them to the pillowcase ragbag. This all seemed a little unnecessary to me.

One of Mama's cleaning specialties was windows. For her windows to pass inspection, the panes had to appear nonexistent. This included the windows between Mama and Daddy's room and the screened front porch. But these same windows, combined with Mama's standard of window perfection, almost caused a tragedy.

After one housecleaning day, Daddy retired to the front porch after supper to relax and read *The Mobile Press*. Mama, reminded of something she wanted to tell him, left her evening habitat, the kitchen, and went to their bedroom to talk to Daddy through the bedroom window. Maybe she wanted to say something to Daddy that little ears did not need to hear. For whatever reason, she tried to stick her head through the window to talk to him. But the sparkling clean window had not been raised; glass shattered and flew everywhere. Mama was covered with blood!

Fortunately, the situation was easily remedied. Mama had only minor wounds on her face and arms, and the glass was easily replaced by the windowpane doctor. Afterward, Daddy loved to joke,

"The windows at our house are so clean, Helen can't tell if they are up or down!"

During the era when I was a teenager (a newly coined word at the time), you might say I wasn't really into housekeeping. Making my bed every day wasn't very important to me, and the week-long, semiannual cleaning affair seemed preposterous. My activities—school, church, and friends—were far more important to me than folded rags and sparkling windows. I was preparing myself for something more important than domestic work!

As a result of my attitude, Mama began to see herself as an unfit mother. Her only daughter did not keep her room clean. When family and friends came to visit, Mama would close my door, shake her head, and say, "I hope I live to see the day she keeps house. I just want to see what her house will look like!"

Well, look at me now. Like Mama, I have a rag-bag (a plastic storage box). And like Mama, I, too, notice fingerprints on windows and French doors. But I reach for the Windex, not the vinegar water. Still, Saint Helen must be proud! Despite my teenage rebellion, Mama's meticulous standards are forever imprinted on my brain.

PICNICS

About the time Mama was eighty, I described to her a wonderful weekend my husband Don and I had spent at Marriott's Grand Hotel and Resort Center on the eastern shore of Mobile Bay. "Since my first visit there years ago, I have felt this place to be enchanted," I shared with her. "When I enter the grounds, I feel like I've entered Fantasy Island. I'm living a fairy tale!"

Mama gave me a sharp look. "Obviously, you don't remember the first time you went to the Grand

Hotel!" In response to my blank stare, she continued. "That's where you took your first steps. You learned to walk on the grounds of the Grand Hotel."

The original hotel building, snuggled under sprawling moss-draped oaks, had long been a landmark, even before my birth. But when fire partially destroyed the structure, my father was called in as a superintendent to help repair and remodel the hotel.

"The job was behind schedule, and Daddy had to be there on Saturdays," Mama explained. (She often referred to her husband as "Daddy" when she was talking to us children.) So Mama loaded the car with bathing suits and towels, quilts, a four-year-old son, a baby daughter who was ready to walk, and a picnic lunch.

Mama described to me in detail those warm, leisurely days. Her children enjoyed splashing in the water and playing on the sandy beach. The shade of massive oaks protected us from the hot sun as my brother and I romped on the grassy lawn and napped on folded quilts. And at lunchtime we had a picnic. Mama could not have picked a more beautiful spot for what was likely my first picnic.

Mama never owned a picnic basket, and the one-red-and-white-checked tablecloth she did have was used on the breakfast room table. But we never missed those picnic necessities because we never had them; we didn't know what a picnic was supposed to look like.

I wish I had memories of those earliest picnics, but I don't. I do remember picnics at the pier in Fairhope, just a few miles north of the Grand Hotel. And I can remember in later years our Saturday picnics en route to Citronelle. Sometimes we stopped beside one of the creeks along Highway 45 or found a shady site next to Sand Ridge Road. The location was less important to hungry kids than the food. Whether the food was fried chicken, potato salad, and oatmeal cookies or something much less exotic, no one ever took a bite until the appointed child recited the blessing:

God is great, God is good
Let us thank Him for our food.
By His hand we are fed,
Thank You, Lord, for daily bread.

The food was the same as what we ate many times in the breakfast room at home. But we were outside and everything seemed magical: The grassy earth was our table, a blue sky was our ceiling, and God's tiniest creatures provided plenty of entertainment.

The eastern shore of the bay and the rural countryside were wonderful places to unpack a lunch, but my favorite picnic spot was in the middle of town, in fact, the very center of downtown Mobile. Bursting with the color of azaleas each spring and cooled by sprawling oaks during hot summer months, Bienville Square was built in the mid-1800s (when it was called City Park), and it became a gathering place during the 1920s, when Mama worked at Gayfer's. To a small child in the 1940s, Bienville Square was a hundred-year-old adventureland to visit each week of the summer.

On Mama's day to go to town—the same day each week—I accompanied her on a variety of errands. This was an era when one went to the gas company to pay the gas bill, the power company to pay for electricity, and the telephone company to pay "Ma Bell." Each office was located downtown. Few families had household checking accounts and "charge card" was an uncoined term. The dentist and the doctor were downtown, too. No one had yet conceived of the shopping mall idea, and we still went to downtown department stores to buy clothing and shoes.

I didn't understand much about paying bills, I was not yet interested in shopping, and I surely did not like doctors or dentists. My favorite part of the trek was our picnic in the park. Some shoppers ate at the lunch counters in Kress, Neisner's, or Woolworth's. Occasionally Mama would give us fifteen cents to buy a hot dog and a Coke, but much more often she packed a picnic lunch.

Mama would pull up to the curb on Dauphin Street across from Gayfer's about the time the store was opening at 9:30 A.M. She'd place a nickel in the parking meter and give the weekly instructions to my older brother and me: "Stay in the square, watch after Dan, and I'll be back in time for lunch." (Dan was our younger brother and the one who needed to be watched most closely.)

We explored every inch of the concrete sidewalks that outlined and crisscrossed the square block area. We watched "millions" of goldfish as they swam in the pool, a reservoir that caught the water spilling from a huge tiered fountain. We used the public restrooms and drank from the public water fountain. When we were tired, we rested on the wrought-iron benches next to old men who read *The Mobile Press* and talked about the war. We were never afraid; we had no reason to be.

Sometimes Mama felt generous and gave us a

nickel before she left for shopping. With that, we would buy a bag of parched peanuts from the vendor in the square; then we'd eat all the peanuts our tummies would hold. We always had peanuts left to feed the squirrel friends that inhabited every inch of Bienville Square. They were tame and would eat from our hands.

Before two hours passed, when the parking meter was ready to expire, Mama returned, often carrying a small package or two. "Come help me get these bags," Mama would call to us as she fed another nickel to the parking meter. She handed her children everything needed for our picnic and then picked a child to say the blessing.

The sandwiches and fruit tasted fresher and the cookies sweeter when they were eaten outside with squirrels playing nearby. Three children thirsty from summer heat and roasted peanuts quickly emptied the thermos of Kool-Aid. Mama knew how to make a picnic lunch, and she knew the perfect place to serve it.

Bienville Square still sits in the center of "Old Mobile." The wrought-iron benches that line the sidewalks are the same ones I sat on when I was a tired little girl. Old men still sit and talk and read *The Mobile Press*. The fountain has been refurbished, but it still spills water twenty-four hours a day into the same surrounding pool. The oak trees are older and more gnarled, with moss sucking life from some of the huge limbs, but they are still home to legions of birds and squirrels. And yes, the "great-grandsquirrels" of my squirrel friends still scamper everywhere, waiting for handouts from peanut bags.

When I remember those long-ago picnics, in my heart I still recite the blessing Mama taught me:

God is great, God is good. . .
Thank You, Lord, for daily bread.

OATMEAL COOKIES

1/2 cup butter

3/4 cup sugar

1 egg

2 tablespoons buttermilk

1 cup flour

1/2 teaspoon baking powder

1/2 teaspoon cinnamon

Salt

1 cup toasted oatmeal

Preheat oven to 350 degrees. Mix ingredients together and drop by spoonfuls on greased cookie sheet. Bake for 10-12 minutes.

(Note: Mama gave a neighbor, Ethel Singley, this recipe in the 1940s. The recipe was returned to me fifty years later by Ethel's daughter, Ann.)

PEACH ICE CREAM

Summertime always brings back memories of peach ice cream, another of Mama's homemade specialties.

I can just see myself, sitting on the wooden steps of the house on Shannon Avenue. I am holding a clear-glass dessert dish, the kind that came in the bottom of the oatmeal box. The dish is filled with peach ice cream, homemade by Mama. Peach was my favorite flavor—and Mama's favorite, too.

When Daddy moved the family to Shannon, Mama wasn't happy about the move, as I've already described. To make amends, Daddy built a wooden frame and planted grapevines in the middle of the right side of the backyard (besides transplanting the fig trees). Then he planted a peach tree in the far corner, next to the fence, beyond the soon-to-be grape arbor. Before many summers passed, Mama was making grape jelly, and the peach tree was producing succulent fruit. Mama used the ripe peaches for the reason they were created—to make peach ice cream.

Ice cream was the weekend dessert at 613 Shannon Avenue fifty-two weeks of the year. In the summertime the family ate this delicacy around the table after Sunday dinner. After church on Sunday night, Mama served ice cream on the screened front porch. The whole family gathered there and sat in darkness. Somehow it seemed a little cooler that way.

The same sweet scene was reenacted when the heat of summer chilled to winter's cold, but then Mama served the night treat in the central hallway. We put chairs there for the weekly ritual. In my earliest memories, the family sat around the heater. Later, we circled the modern floor furnace, of which we were justly proud. We didn't talk much. We just ate our ice cream and savored every bite.

Milk, eggs, and sugar were plentiful (except during the war, when we had problems getting sugar). A big bottle of Watkins vanilla flavoring always seemed to be on hand. And every Saturday, Mama's agenda included ice cream preparation.

She cooked the custard, beat it, and then something else was added. I'm not sure, but I think she folded in stiffly beaten egg whites. When the mixture was complete, she poured it into a double-width aluminum ice tray. The tray came with the Frigidaire, and we normally used it for ice cubes—except on Saturday; then it became the ice cream tray.

This tray was only twice the size of my ice trays, and I often wonder how Mama managed to eke ten or more servings out of such a small container. We always had full bowls. Of course, if we had company, Mama usually wasn't very hungry, or she'd say she would have "just a bite of ice cream."

Once a new product called Junket appeared on the grocery store shelves. The advertising touted it as the new way to make homemade ice cream without all the cooking and beating. Mama tried it once or twice; Daddy soon pronounced it "junk" instead of "Junket." The boxes of powdery substance disappeared from our house, and Mama returned to her Saturday cooking and beating.

One afternoon on his way home from work, Daddy bought an ice cream freezer. It might have been on the market for a while, but the first one Daddy saw, he bought. The Sears and Roebuck freezer had a wooden tub and a gallon-and-a-half metal container inside. Mama packed it with the right combination of ice cream custard, ice, and ice cream salt, and then she turned with a crank while a small child sat on top; to our amazement, it produced about three times the amount of ice cream I had ever seen in one place in my entire life.

Mama continued her Saturday ritual, except the ice cream was now frozen on the back porch and served immediately. The children usually ate their Saturday bowl on the wooden back steps while Daddy and Mama ate in the kitchen. For the first time ever, Mama offered seconds. She poured the remaining frozen mixture into the same aluminum tray and saved it in the freezer for the Sunday delight.

Baskin-Robbins could have opened their stores with our list of family flavors. Of course, there was chocolate, Daddy's favorite, and vanilla. In season, we had fresh strawberry. We had banana, lemon, walnut, and toasted pecan. Someone gave Mama a recipe for coffee ice cream and she tried it, but only once. It, too, went the way of Junket! But when late June or early July came, we had peach ice cream from the first Saturday the peaches were ripe until the last peaches were picked.

I've looked for ice cream recipes in all of Mama's files. I haven't found anything that dates back as far as my childhood, except for a vanilla ice cream recipe. I suspect she made vanilla every week and then added ingredients that made it look like and taste like its name.

Summertime. . .and I want to eat peach ice cream from a clear-glass bowl, sitting on the glider in the screened front porch at 613 Shannon Avenue. I don't care what the nutritionists think. I know it would be good for my heart. After all, Mama always did know what was best for me.

FRIED OYSTERS

Fried oysters were like almost everything else Mama cooked—they were good. But she only prepared them in the "R" months.

According to Mama, the "R" months are September through April, those months that contain the letter R in their names. Not coincidentally, they also are the cool months in our steamy state of Alabama. That's why these months are a good time to serve extremely perishable oysters.

The first chill of September found Daddy

headed south after his workday ended. The drive to Bayou La Batre, oyster capital of Mobile and surrounding counties, took about an hour. When the freshest oysters in the bayou town had been located and purchased, Daddy headed north and home.

According to my source, Mr. Dan Thompson, Sr., a bushel of oysters cost fifty cents in the 1940s. But that same bushel yielded about a thousand times that amount in culinary pleasure, especially if the oysters were unfortunate enough to be dropped into Mama's "just hot enough" grease.

As soon as Daddy finished supper we could find him behind the garage opening the oysters. "Shucking" is the proper term used today for removing the edible delicacy from the rough and dirty shells. Daddy always called it "openin' oysters." If I could slip out of the house without being noticed—and I usually could—I stood beside him as he opened shell after shell and dumped the contents into a gallon container. I was fascinated; he could insert his oyster knife into a nonexistent opening and with one twist of the wrist display the slimy glob, which would be devoured as a delicacy within the next twenty-four hours.

Daddy was a taster and a teaser. We suspected he consumed a significant number of raw oysters during the two-hour or longer "openin' " session. Of course he always teased that he was going to teach me to eat raw oysters, too.

I must have been about seven or eight the night I decided I would give in to Daddy's gentle persuasion. Daddy said I should just swallow the oyster whole, that no chewing was necessary. And he was right. The oyster only touched my tongue, and then it was gone, skidding down my throat and into my tummy. There was no time to taste or chew. On that particular maiden voyage, as I remember, my oyster traveled up just as fast as it traveled down.

Fortunately, despite that experience, fried oysters, especially Mama's fried oysters, remained one of my favorite meals. Whenever she served oysters, Mama fried at least a quart of them. When relatives were invited, she might fry a gallon of the tasty morsels. The last oyster taken from the hot grease was just as golden brown as the first one off the skillet.

It is no easy task to fry good oysters. And the more oysters you fry, the more difficult it becomes. Each oyster dropped into hot grease leaves a little of its cornmeal coating, which then settles to the bottom, turns brown, and sometimes burns. But if Daddy were a craftsman as he shucked, Mama was an artist as she fried. She said the secret was the temperature of the grease (known today as oil).

Mama never owned an electric frying pan. She fried her oysters in the skillet Daddy bought for her in 1931, the year they were married. Deeper than a regular skillet, she always called this particular one the "deep skillet." Only one of its many tasks was to fry perfect oysters.

"The grease has to be just right," Mama always said when she was preparing to fry oysters. "It has to be hot enough, but not too hot."

Mama fried skillet after skillet of oysters in the same grease. Each was cooked to perfection, crispy and well done, but never burned. She removed them carefully from the grease, individually, and placed them on a brown paper bag to drain. When she was convinced "every ounce" of grease had drained from the oyster, she quickly put it into the roaster, which was sitting in the warm oven.

Skillet after skillet of oysters were fried until the roaster was nearly full. Mama served them with potato salad, loaf bread, iced tea—and a pound cake when company came. A tall bottle of Heinz tomato ketchup always stood in the middle of the table.

Mama stored the oysters that survived the first meal in the refrigerator overnight; they made a wonderful lunch the next day. She warmed them in the oven, and then we covered them with ketchup and placed them between two slices of loaf bread. We called it an "oyster sandwich," and it was more wonderful than the fancy "oyster loaf" invented many years later.

Today when I fry oysters, the oysters and the kitchen are always a mess. But I always did, and still do, one thing right. I only fry oysters in the "R" months! Mama's most important lessons still weave together the fabric of my life.

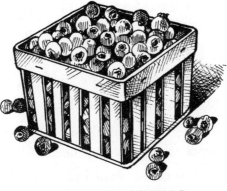

BLUEBERRY THING

The two-and-one-half-mile walk from his house to the blueberry farm was quite a trek for five-year-old Henry. He held tightly to the hand of his older sister Sallie as his legs flew, making two steps for every one of hers. The damp, early morning dew made sand stick to his bare feet.

The blueberry farm was near the road, which was more like a wagon trail, that led to Mobile, Alabama. Years later this thoroughfare would be paved and named US Highway 45; it would connect the southern United States to the Great Lakes.

But for now, this was Henry's first trip to the blueberry farm. He had waited impatiently for the time to arrive when he could walk to the farm, pick blueberries, and earn his first money. His excitement grew as he approached the sprawling plantation house built by the Cooper family from up north. Other pickers who had arrived earlier waited under large oak trees that shaded the home. Henry soon found himself in the midst of a group of all ages and sizes as they followed the overseer to an area of the farm where berries were ripe and waiting to be picked.

The sun that morning quickly became almost unbearable for young Henry, but he did not complain. After lunch a dark cloud gave false hope for an afternoon shower that would have brought some relief from the heat. Sallie soon found a shaded area where her young brother could nap while she continued to pick the ripe, succulent berries.

Late in the evening the berries were carefully

poured into baskets and readied for shipping. Tomorrow the train would make its weekly stop at Russell, the last stop before Citronelle, to pick up the produce. Henry's berries would be traveling to market in the North.

The Whatley children headed west out Sand Ridge Road, which was not yet named, retracing the route they had traveled earlier in the day. Henry was tired, but he was excited! He tightly clutched his day's wages in his pocket: a shiny quarter.

Today was the beginning of a dream for Henry. "When I get big, I am going to buy the blueberry farm!" he announced grandly.

That year was 1906. A few years later, following the premature deaths of his parents, young Henry was on his own. At fifteen, he cooked for the railroad crews at Russell, and just two years later he worked for the same railroad at the shops in Whistler. He married, started a family, and built houses. Henry saved his money and bought property in the area of his birth. But the blueberry farm was considered "heir property," and as such it was tied up in court.

As a child I remember my father, the grown-up Henry, keeping his dream alive. He told me about all the years he walked to the farm season after season and about the shiny quarters he earned. And he always said, "Someday I will buy that land!"

In 1951 the property titles were finally cleared. The land was for sale, but Daddy was not the only one who wanted it.

Daddy was known locally for his "deals." While others were fretting, hiring lawyers, and fighting, Daddy made one of his famous deals, and his dream came true. He bought the blueberry farm.

The plantation house had burned to the ground many years earlier, and only the brick chimney remained to mark the spot. The well where young Henry had drawn cool water to drink had been abandoned. The flowers that once surrounded the house were overrun with weeds and no longer bloomed. But the blueberry bushes remained, and many were as tall as trees now. They had not been cultivated for many years, yet they had reached through the underbrush for sunshine, soaked up rainwater from the sandy soil, and flourished!

Summer came and those bushes were covered with the most tantalizing berries a twelve-year-old girl had ever tasted. Maybe I was intoxicated by the stories Daddy had told me over the years or by the realization that some dreams do come true. But Mama viewed the blueberry bushes from a different perspective. Having lived through the Great Depression and experienced the scarcity of food, she did not want anything edible to perish. All those blueberry bushes were a real challenge to her, especially since they were thirty miles from where we lived.

Our family made regular trips to the newly acquired property to pick the berries. They were eaten, canned, frozen, and shared with others. After four years of regular berry-picking trips, the family moved to the property. Mama could then walk right out her back door and pick her berries.

The most likely use for all those blueberries was blueberry pie. Everyone who tasted hers knew that Mama didn't need to enter a contest to see who could make the best pie; Mama's pie was the standard by which all others would be judged. She deserved the blueberry pie blue ribbon award without ever entering a contest!

But to Mama, hers was just an ordinary blueberry pie. She started the pie by washing the fresh berries. "Don't wash the berries when you pick them," Mama said. "They lose their flavor if you do. Use them before you put them in the refrigerator if you can. They taste better that way."

Mama handled the berries with love. She removed those that were too ripe and any tiny stems that might still be attached. Once they were washed, she covered them with sugar and set them aside while she mixed the crust.

If anything were more famous locally than

Mama's blueberry pie, it was her piecrust. This was real piecrust—Mrs. Helen Whatley's homemade piecrust—not to be confused with graham cracker or store-bought crusts.

Mama never measured, but she always seemed to have just the right amount of flour in the bowl. Then she added just the right amount of shortening. She cut the shortening with a fork and added ice water—and she always ended up with a flaky crust that was strong enough not to tear, yet tender enough to melt in your mouth.

When Mama was living, I often asked her "how much" when we talked about a recipe. She had a standard answer: "Enough. You will know when it is enough."

When the dough was just the right consistency, Mama covered the new yellow chrome dinette table with Cut-Rite wax paper. Then she "turned-out" the dough to be rolled. Mama never owned a rolling pin, nor did she ever want or need one. She sprinkled the dough with flour and rolled it with a quart-glass milk bottle. The dough had to be smooth and just the right thickness to earn Mama's approval.

Once Mama was satisfied, she carefully placed the bottom crust in a Pyrex pie plate. Then she piled it high with sugarcoated berries that she dotted with butter. She repeated the rolling ritual to prepare a top pastry, a cover for the berries. Now Mama demonstrated her artistic abilities as she fluted the two crusts tightly together and dotted the dough with a fork she had dipped in the flour.

In her lifetime, Mama must have made a million blueberry pies!

When she was somewhere between seventy-five and eighty years old and about ready to start on her second million, "The Blueberry Thing" appeared. Elizabeth King, a friend of hers with whom she shared berries each summer, gave her the recipe.

The recipe called for a simple crust of flour, margarine, and chopped pecans. A mixture of cream cheese and confectioner's sugar came next, to be topped with a layer of cooked fresh blueberries. Cool Whip, piled high, was the crowning touch. With just a little bit of help, any ten-year-old could make this dessert. I've made my share. For lack of a better term, I call the concoction "The Blueberry Thing," but it could never be confused with the *real* blueberry thing, Mama's homemade blueberry pie.

I wish I knew how much flour, salt, and short-ening Mama used to make her pie. And how much ice water. That seems to be the biggest problem, the ice water. I still can't decide how much is "enough." But sometimes in other areas of my life, I remember what Mama said: "You'll know when it is enough." I do my best to follow her advice.

BLUEBERRY PIE FILLING
(the *real* blueberry thing)

4 cups fresh blueberries, rinsed
Sugar
1–2 tablespoons cornstarch
Butter

Place berries in medium pot, add sugar, and cook over low heat until berries come to a boil.

Cook about five minutes and then add cornstarch.

When the mixture is completely cooled, fill unbaked pie shell. Dot with butter.

Cut second crust into one-inch-wide strips for basket-weave top crust.

Bake at 350 degrees until crust is lightly browned.

PLAIN PASTRY (PIECRUST)

2 cups flour
1 1/2 teaspoons salt
1/3 cup shortening
4–6 tablespoons ice water

Mix and sift flour and salt. Cut in shortening with a fork. Add only enough water to hold the ingredients together.

Chill thoroughly. Divide dough in two parts and roll out on a lightly floured surface. Line a pie pan with half the pastry. Pinch pastry with fingers to make a fancy edge and prick the bottom and sides with a fork. Bake in very hot oven, 450 degrees, for 10–15 minutes. For a double-crust pie, line pan with pastry and put in filling, cover with top crust, and bake as directed.

BLUEBERRY DELIGHT
("The Blueberry Thing")
(from Elizabeth King)

Crust

1 stick margarine, melted

1 cup flour

1 cup finely chopped pecans

Mix together ingredients and pat in 9– x 13–inch baking dish to make crust. Bake at 325 degrees for 20 minutes. Cool.

Filling

2 8–ounce packages cream cheese, softened

2 cups confectioner's sugar

1 teaspoon vanilla extract

Mix together ingredients and spread over crust.

Cover with cooked fresh blueberries or pie filling. Top with Cool Whip. Cool 12 hours and then cut into squares to serve.

GARDEN

I was born in the city. We always had hot water, indoor plumbing, and a washing machine. And outdoors we always had a garden.

Mama loved her garden. When any opportunity presented itself, she would always say, "I just love to watch things grow!"

Some things were understood. For instance, a robin was not the first sign of spring—the smell of freshly tilled soil was. The smell of insecticides followed quickly, and not so much later, we breathed the fragrance of peas and butter beans boiling in a pot.

The gardens at 613 Shannon Avenue grew annually for fifteen or more years. They moved with Mama when she moved to the country to live, and there they grew into even bigger gardens. She carried on her garden affair there for thirty-plus years.

About the time Mama turned seventy-five years old, she started making announcements. Those announcements were just as annual as the planting of the garden. She always made them on January first, when she was surrounded by her extended family for her New Year's Day celebration. With a solemn look on her face and an air of sadness, she would announce, "I'm not having a garden this year."

Everyone agreed that she shouldn't. A garden was too much work for a seventy-five-year-old, or an eighty-nine-year-old, or whatever birthday it was that Mama was planning to celebrate on January sixth.

We all discussed in depth the reasons for not having a garden: "It will be hot by summertime, too hot to be outside working in a garden"; "It might not rain enough, or it could be like last year and rain too much"; "The bugs seem to be getting worse every year, and even spraying doesn't keep them away"; "Vegetables can be bought more cheaply than they can be raised." We were all in complete agreement.

By February, though, Mama would have reconsidered. Maybe she would have just a few tomato plants. In March, she would add squash and peas, but only two rows of each. In less than three months, Mama's plan for no garden became a plan for a small truck farm.

She'd make several trips to the local hardware store, where she would discuss with the employees the varieties of vegetables she planned to grow. She didn't really need their advice. They probably had never planted a real garden. But it was a nice place to visit and a nice subject to discuss while she waited for her soil to get warm enough for planting. And when her seed purchases were all complete, Mama needed only to consult her *Farmer's Almanac* and decide on a date to plant the garden.

For more than twenty-five years my family— Don, the boys, and I—traveled twenty-five miles to Mama's house every Saturday afternoon for a visit and our best meal of the week. Our April visits were always an adventure. By then the garden had been planted.

"Come and see the garden before you go inside," Mama would say excitedly as she met us at the car. We followed her around the garage to the fenced area that enclosed a plot that was always larger than we expected. Before we could speak, however, Mama would explain, as usual, that the garden had turned out bigger than she had planned for it to be. We only saw neat rows of dirt, but Mama saw much more. She had a vision of fully grown plants loaded with ripening vegetables! On subsequent Saturday visits we, too, would see what Mama had visualized earlier. The neat rows of brown dirt would be dotted, then covered with plants, bushes, and vines, until we had little space to walk between the rows.

Warm spring mornings quickly gave way to the hot days of June and July. Still, Mama remained committed to her garden. She went early to the garden while the ground was still moist from the dew. And she was always dressed appropriately.

Mama did occasionally wear pants, but never in the garden. Her oldest housedresses were designated each season as garden attire. If the dresses did not have long sleeves, she would cover her arms with a long-sleeved blouse or shirt that she'd wear over her neatly ironed print dress. A floppy straw hat, with fabric strings attached to secure it beneath her chin, completed her garden outfit.

Early in the morning, thus properly attired, she made her daily pilgrimage from the back door of the house to the garden gate, a distance of about a hundred feet. She went at least once every day, from the day the soil was tilled until the last pod of okra was cut and the last tomato picked. When there was no work to do, Mama would just stand and watch the garden grow.

We all knew it was too hot for her to hoe, water, weed, spray, pick, pull, and whatever else she did in the garden. But we also knew that she would surely die if she could not hoe, water, weed, spray, pick, and pull. For Mama the garden was therapeutic. "It just makes me feel better when I can watch something grow," she would say.

She did not pass on to her daughter her gene for gardening. My definition of the great outdoors is the space between the back door of my house and the front door of my car. Fortunately, her older son either enjoyed the annual garden adventure or at least he cooperated with it. His work made the garden possible.

At least once in her lifetime Mama planted

almost everything that grows, from radishes to gourds. She planted at least three kinds of peas—butter, English, and regular—and two kinds of beans —butter and pole. She always had her beloved squash and okra, plus cucumbers for her pickles. Besides all that, there was the corn, sometimes sweet corn and sometimes field corn. Occasionally she planted eggplant, onions—green or white—and peppers, sometimes hot and sometimes not.

But Mama always planted tomatoes. Homegrown tomatoes were her gardening trademark. For Mama, there was something holy about bringing food out of the damp, rich earth. But the most sacred thing that grew in any garden, according to Mama, was a tomato.

TOMATOES

Mabel, my longtime friend and my short-time neighbor, knocked on my back door a few days ago. She carried in her arms homegrown tomatoes from the garden in her backyard. As soon as she left, I made a bacon, lettuce, and tomato sandwich on white bread covered with mayonnaise.

Obviously, this was not a day to count fat grams. This was, however, my first real tomato since Mama died four years ago. The sandwich was wonderful, especially the homegrown tomato.

Real tomatoes are grown by friends—or by Mama. Those labeled "homegrown" at the supermarket, produce stand, or even the truck parked by the side of the road, do not qualify. They probably have been shipped from somewhere far away; they have hard green centers and taste like wood. Homegrown, however, means they have been cared for lovingly; they probably were watched from the kitchen window as they ripened.

Some think tomatoes are tomatoes, but I know they are divided into three categories: shipped, homegrown, and Mama's homegrown. Just a few short months before her death, Mama was picking tomatoes from the two rows she had grown behind her house.

Some years she bought and planted seeds in milk cartons. These she placed in her den window, hoping that the sunlight and inside warmth would encourage them to sprout early. Other years she purchased young plants from the local hardware store. Only when Mama was certain the last cold spell had passed did she place her precious tomato plants in the outside soil.

Mama wanted her tomatoes to be perfect. To be sure that the end product met her standards, she would stick, prune, and water. (Sticking, which requires long narrow sticks of wood and also long narrow strips of fabric, ensures that through varying stages of ripening, the plants will remain erect. Then the tomatoes won't touch the soil and spoil.) Mama picked the ripened produce at what she called the "right moment." This was always early morning. She carefully placed each tomato in a container with other tomatoes and brought it to the den, where newspapers had been spread on the carpeted floor. Then she used a soft cloth to lovingly wipe every tomato and remove any trace of sand.

Mama had a way of grading produce: First, she set aside for her own use any tomatoes with imperfections. Next, she gave the larger, more perfect ones to others, and she made the deliveries herself in her 1968 Cutlass Oldsmobile. At least once each week she made the four-mile trip to Citronelle so she could deliver tomatoes. And each Thursday the trip was the twenty-five miles to Mobile, en route to the beauty shop and grocery store, delivering more tomatoes on her way.

Mama never said much about sharing. She just did it. I got a call from her every Wednesday night. "How many tomatoes do you need?" My friends would tell me she had brought tomatoes to them, too. Once a friend of mine asked me a question that did not need an answer: "Did your mother leave some tomatoes on my back steps? I think they're from her because it is Thursday."

Each and every Thursday Mama would leave brown bags filled with tomatoes at my house. She printed the name of the recipient on each bag in bold Magic Marker—in other words, the person to whom I should deliver it. She always called a few days later to be certain I had done what I had been instructed to do. (When she died I was fifty-one years old—but she still thought I was a child of ten, a person whom she needed to check up on frequently.)

Mama thought tomatoes had three purposes. The first, of course, was to share. The second was to enjoy. She loved a ripe tomato. (She always peeled tomatoes before serving them, and she never liked the fact that I didn't.) Each year as she consumed more acid than her body could tolerate, she developed a rash on her neck and arms. But she would not stop eating tomatoes. Rather, she did what she thought was more sensible. She treated the rash. But all the sharing and eating did not deplete her supply, which brings me to the third purpose—to save. Mama was always grieved if anything was wasted, especially food, and more especially, tomatoes.

So she cooked okra and tomatoes, and she stewed tomatoes for the freezer. She even cooked and froze tomatoes for my freezer. She made tomato relish, pickled green tomatoes, and tomato anything that anyone recommended. She was frying green tomatoes before they even built the Whistle Stop Cafe, made famous in the novel and film *Fried Green Tomatoes.*

How I wish I had understood the significance of those paper bags of tomatoes! How I wish I had kept just one with "Barbara" printed boldly with Magic Marker—in Mama's hand. No wonder she thought tomatoes were sacred. In her mind, those red, juicy globes were the same as love.

SATURDAY NIGHT SUPPER

In the morning we sometimes have brunch instead of breakfast. Even if we call it breakfast, it is not always a "real" breakfast. Often it is a bagel with cream cheese or simply a banana. Then we likely call our noon meal lunch, the same name given to food we carry any time of the day in a picnic basket or brown bag. At night we have dinner, while our older rural-born relatives are eating supper.

But Mama knew the real names of all the meals. Breakfast was first, early every morning, and it always included biscuits. Dinner was at noon and consisted of soup or a sandwich (the choice being determined by the outside temperature). Supper was about five o'clock in the evening, when Daddy got home and the cornbread was done.

"I just love to cook!" I must have heard Mama make that statement a thousand times. She was a blue-ribbon cook, trained young by Aunt Peggy, and she had many years of practice. But when Daddy died in 1962, Mama amended her statement, adding, "And I don't have enough people to cook for anymore."

For the next twenty-five years Mama cooked supper every Saturday night for my family. She said it was the highlight of her week. She was still cooking on Saturday night at eighty-nine years old, just nine weeks before her death. Her preparation began on Thursday evening—no quick casserole recipes for Mama—and it concluded late on Saturday night when the last dish was dried and placed in the proper cabinet. Saturday night supper was not just a meal; it was an event!

When Mama came for her every-Thursday overnight visit, she asked her every-Thursday question: "What time are you coming for supper Saturday?" But her voice included no question mark. She really wasn't asking if we were coming; she only needed to know the exact time we would arrive.

By Thursday she had chosen the entree, leaving Friday for grocery shopping. On Thursday night Mama would always discuss with herself what she would add to the roast to complete our supper meal on Saturday night. Rice and gravy were a given. "Daddy always wanted rice and gravy when we had roast," she reminded us frequently. Occasionally, at a grandson's request, Mama would fry chicken or fish or make one of her famous chicken pies with real homemade crust. However, we were usually safe to assume that Saturday's meal would be roast. Mama rarely bought the more expensive cuts of beef, however. She would buy sirloin tip or rump roast only if it were a store special that week, but she usually purchased chuck.

Early on Saturday Mama seared the roast in the preheated deep skillet. The meat was covered with seasonings and placed in the oven in the same skillet—or Dutch oven, as Mama called it. "Add just a little bit of water to the bottom of the skillet," she said when she was teaching me the tricks of the trade.

Mama cooked vegetables in season—squash, green beans, peas, okra, turnip greens, butter beans, sweet potatoes, and corn. If these vegetables were not in season, they could easily be found in the freezer. Prior to our arrival, she cooked two or more vegetables, and we'd find the pots that held them on the electric stove.

The salads—green, carrot, pear, potato, congealed, or slaw—would be all ready, waiting in the refrigerator. Often more than one of these would make its way to the Saturday night table. And of course Mama served fresh, homegrown sliced tomatoes every Saturday, from the week the first tomatoes ripened until late in the fall. Her kitchen table was covered with a printed oilcloth, and on it we'd find jars of homemade pickles or tomato relish, and sometimes both. Occasionally Mama would surprise us with homemade yeast rolls made from her mother's old recipe.

The dessert, usually prepared on Friday night, sat on the tabletop hot water heater that served as a countertop next to the stove. Dessert might be blackberry or blueberry pie, depending on the season. Strawberries were a June favorite, especially if they were served over homemade pound cake and topped with ice cream. Mama served freshly baked pecan, potato, and mincemeat pies and occasionally an apple cake made with fresh apples. But if her favorite (and only) son-in-law were on her mind or in her heart, Mama made a homemade chocolate pie. We always knew what to expect for Saturday dessert when Mama asked, "Don, do you know what we are having for dessert today?" The answer to that question would always be chocolate pie.

If we arrived later than the expected time, Mama would be watching and listening for our car. We always drove around the house and parked near the pecan trees in the backyard. When Mama thought the leaves or pollen would damage the car paint, she would come out the back door onto the concrete steps and tell Don to move the car. Of course, he always did. In fact, we all tried to do everything she told us to do.

A tantalizing aroma would greet us as we opened the doors of the car. The delicious smell of roast cooking in the oven filtered through the open back door almost every Saturday afternoon.

It was Saturday and it was roast.

When possible, we arrived early in the after-noon. We picked blackberries in the spring and blueberries a little later in the summer. We watched the garden grow, and when the vegetables were ready, we shelled peas and snapped beans. In the fall we went to the fields, the site of the old Cooper plantation and blueberry farm, to pick pecans from the same trees that had provided nuts for the Cooper family almost a hundred years earlier.

Sometimes Mama would take the boys down to the ponds in the woods behind the house. Their grandfather, whom the older one vaguely remembered and the younger one never knew, had built three fish ponds even before the home was built in 1955. He wanted Mama to have a place to fish any time she chose.

By later in the afternoon everyone gathered inside. The boys watched football or other ball games on television with their father as I sat at the kitchen table and worked on a variety of projects. Sometimes I made posters for Mama's Sunday school class or Christmas party invitations for the annual children's party at church. Late Saturday afternoon might find the rest of us doing a variety of things, but not Mama. Every Saturday was the same. She was on a mission!

She was always in one of three places in the kitchen: either in front of the stove, in front of the sink, or walking in between. She would be cooking rice, making the gravy, mixing the bread, and warming the numerous pots of food she had prepared earlier.

In addition to the vast array of food, two items were standard at those Saturday meals: cornbread just removed from the oven and the blessing. Everyone knew to have his or her hands washed before the cornbread was done, and we never took a bite before the food was blessed.

Mama never let me help with the cooking. She would sometimes ask me to slice the roast, and she always asked me to get the ice. After the meal she handed a sponge to me and asked me to wipe the table. These were jobs she thought I might be capable of handling, but she always wiped the table again, just to make sure it was clean. (After all, remember, she thought I was really still about ten.)

Only twice have I seen a display of food like the one Mama served every Saturday. The first time was at Mrs. Wilkes's Boarding House in Savannah, Georgia. Mrs. Wilkes had everything Mama had, including hot cornbread and the blessing (offered by Mr. Wilkes), every day at 11:30 sharp. The second occasion was so touching I could hardly enjoy the meal; I was missing Mama too much. Mrs. Ada Pearl Maxwell, of Grand Bay, Alabama, invited me to her house for Monday lunch. She is a distant family member of my parents' generation, and we talked family history. Her rural home was built the same year Daddy built Mama's country home. When I walked through her front door it looked and smelled just like Mama's house.

Miss Ada Pearl had a big kitchen with a chrome

table. She covered that table with the same kind of food I had eaten every Saturday of my adult life until Mama died. We had the blessing and we had hot cornbread. And she wouldn't let me help with the food, but she did let me get the ice. She let me wipe the table with a sponge when the meal was finished. And then she wiped it again, just like Mama had.

The rest of the world thought it was noon on Monday. But I knew it was Saturday night, time for one last meal at Mama's house, one last blessing.

LILLIE'S HOMEMADE ROLLS

1 pint sweetened condensed milk
1/2 cup mashed potatoes
1 teaspoon salt
1/2 teaspoon baking soda
1/4 cup lukewarm water
1/2 cup sugar
1/2 cup shortening, melted
1 yeast cake
1 teaspoon baking powder

Scald milk and cool. When lukewarm, add potatoes. Combine salt, baking soda, baking powder, and yeast that has been dissolved in lukewarm water with shortening and enough flour to make a sponge. Let stand until light, and then add enough flour to make a dough. Knead thoroughly and place in a greased bowl. Cover and place in the "ice box." Use after 24 hours. Let rolls rise in pan until double in bulk, from one to three hours. Bake at 450 degrees for 15–20 minutes. Dough will keep in the refrigerator for a week. Makes about five dozen medium rolls.

(Note: This recipe was handed down to Mama from her mother, Lillie.)

APPLE CAKE

(from Mrs. Beatrice Reynolds)

1¹/₄ cups oil

2 cups sugar

3 eggs, well beaten

3 cups fresh apples, chopped

1 cup pecans, chopped

3 cups plain flour

1 teaspoon baking soda

1 teaspoon salt

2 teaspoons vanilla extract

Grease and lightly flour two nine-inch baking pans. Mix the oil with the sugar. Add the eggs. Combine apples and pecans and add to the oil, sugar, and egg mixture. Stir in flour, baking soda, and salt. Add vanilla extract. Pour apple cake batter in baking pans. Put in a cold oven and bake at 300 degrees for about 45 minutes.

Icing

1 1/2 cups light or dark brown sugar
1 1/2 sticks margarine
1/4 + 1/8 cup evaporated milk
1 teaspoon vanilla extract

Melt margarine and add sugar until dissolved. Add evaporated milk and let come to a full boil. Remove from heat and let cool until icing is at spreading consistency. Add one teaspoon vanilla to icing and proceed to spread on cake.

(Note: This recipe was given to Mama by the mother of Reverend Louie Reynolds, Mama's pastor during the 1960s.)

CHOCOLATE PIE

$1/2$ cup cocoa

1 cup sugar

$1/3$ cup cornstarch

$1/4$ teaspoon salt

3 cups milk

3 tablespoons butter

$1^{1}/2$ teaspoons vanilla extract

Combine cocoa, sugar, cornstarch, and salt.

Blend in milk one cup at a time. Cook over medium heat, stirring constantly, until mixture comes to a boil.

Boil one minute. Remove from heat and blend in butter and vanilla extract. Pour into baked piecrust and cover with plastic wrap. Cool, then chill. Top with whipped topping or meringue.

THANKSGIVING PIES

The air is crisp and smells like cinnamon. In the Deep South, the leaves are turning, and turkeys are becoming an endangered species. It's time to buy the cranberry sauce and plan the menu for Thanksgiving dinner. In Mobile the holiday season has arrived and will not end until Ash Wednesday. Thanksgiving, Christmas, New Year's Day, and Mardi Gras all give our family reason to gather, enjoy good food, and enjoy each other.

Before Daddy's death, the Thanksgiving gathering

was always held at Mama's house. Fall months are for hunting, and Thanksgiving was a day for the men to hunt deer. But by noon the hunters would return for the midday feast and a short time of visiting with the relatives. Often they managed to slip out again after lunch to assess the wildlife situation one more time.

After Daddy's death, however, Mama rarely hosted the Thanksgiving gathering, and Don and I inherited the privilege of having the celebration in our home. Besides our family, we invite friends who do not have family nearby (or are not close to their family), as well as friends who have lost their spouses. One invitation grants lifetime membership to all future celebrations. At each gathering, we give everyone the date and host name for the next event. For Thanksgiving the total count sometimes climbs to twenty-five.

By six A.M. the turkey fills our home with a wonderful aroma. We adorn the tables with the best china, crystal, and silver, as well as autumn center-pieces and candles. Placecards (made for many years by the children) indicate the seating arrangement.

Guests bring specialty dishes to complement the turkey, dressing, gravy, and rolls that Don and I have prepared. They bring fresh corn, squash casse-role, salads, and other delicacies for which they are known. But not Mama. Every year her Thanksgiving contribution arrived in Pyrex pie plates, usually six but sometimes more.

The composition of the pie menu did not just happen. Rather, it was the result of a scientific survey made by Mama in October. She always polled the male family members to determine what kinds of pies she should make to serve on Thanksgiving Day.

It was important to Mama that she bake each man's favorite. She revised her list weekly as some changed their minds. When the list was compiled, revised, and recompiled, and there was no time left for anyone to change his mind, Mama went grocery shopping. She knew without asking which store had the best price on mincemeat, Hershey's cocoa, and canned pumpkin.

She also knew who had the freshest coconut.

Keep in mind that none of the men ever asked for coconut pie. But I knew Mama would bring at least one coconut pie to my house every Thanksgiving morning. Coconut is my favorite pie.

Mama did not believe in canned, boxed, or even frozen coconut. I suspect she might have been more likely to compromise a religious conviction than to use anything other than fresh coconut. And nothing other than "real" coconut (Mama's word for fresh) ever found its way into one of her cream pies.

Mama checked out the brown hairy globes in the grocery stores. She would hold each ugly ball first with one hand and then with the other as if she were calculating its weight. She shook it and listened. She examined the end, or the "eyes," which somehow enlightened her as to whether or not it might be ripe. Selecting and purchasing the prize coconut was the first step in making the pie she knew to be her daughter's favorite.

Gadgets may be sold today to crack coconuts, but Mama took hers outside and cracked them with a hammer. When the hard shell was shattered, Mama took the pieces inside to begin the next step in the lengthy coconut pie process.

On the Monday before Thanksgiving—never Sunday or Tuesday—Mama baked the piecrusts for the cream pies. Tuesday was always the day to cook custards and bake the pumpkin pie. Wednesday was reserved for pies with two crusts and the meringue for the custard pies.

"I just don't understand why this meringue failed," Mama said every Thanksgiving morning. Naturally, she had a high standard for her meringue. Standing tall and lightly browned, her meringues looked wonderful to me. But Mama was never satisfied with wonderful. She always wanted perfect!

On Thanksgiving morning Mama delivered the pies to my house, where she placed them on the dessert table and very carefully cut them into eight pieces each. Mama took excellent care of everything she created, especially her pies. We served the freshly baked pies following the noon meal.

Ball games, pie, current handwork projects, more pie, and plenty of hot coffee—always served with pie —filled the afternoons. Some people would leave, others would come by, usually for pie. The evening meal was turkey sandwiches and one final slice of pie.

Mama made sure that there would be enough of each kind of pie to serve to everyone who wanted a piece. This presented some dilemmas when nightfall came, one piece was left, and two people wanted that single slice. One year we appeared to have a serious pie crisis. Only one lopsided piece of chocolate pie was left at the end of the day, and two family members pretended to want that particular pie. Mama was distraught and promised to bring two chocolate pies for the next Thanksgiving celebration. But after much negotiation and laughter, the truth became clear: The two chocolate pie contenders were both as stuffed as the early morning turkey and neither of them could eat it. The single slice was left uneaten, a silent testimony to Mama's uncanny ability to provide more than enough of everyone's favorite.

The past fifteen years have brought changes. We have less family and we eat less dessert. But the tradition continues. After all, holidays are meant for sharing. If you don't get a better invitation, don't spend your day alone—come to our celebration. We just need to know how to spell your name for the placecard and a little time to find another plate.

COCONUT CREAM PIE

1 cup sugar

4 tablespoons cornstarch

3 egg yolks (reserve egg whites)

2 cups milk

1½ cups coconut

1 teaspoon vanilla extract

2 tablespoons margarine, melted

Blend sugar and cornstarch. Beat the egg yolks slightly and add to sugar mixture. Add sugar, coconut, and milk. Cook over low heat until mixture has thickened. Add vanilla extract and melted margarine and pour into a homemade crust (see pie-crust recipe, page 121).

Top with stiffly beaten egg whites with a little sugar added after they are stiff. Bake in a 300-degree oven for about 15 minutes, or until lightly browned.

(Note: Although I know Mama might not approve, you have my permission to use frozen coconut and cook the custard in the microwave, high power, stirring every two to three minutes until thickened. A "homemade" piecrust may be one bought in the dairy case at your local supermarket.)

RULES

At church Mama had another name. She was Mrs. Whatley.

Mrs. Whatley taught six-year-old children for forty-five consecutive years. She did not have an education degree or a high school diploma, yet she was an outstanding teacher. She was educated by master teachers, denominational literature, and every child she taught. Her classes were for one hour each week, on Sunday, in Sunday school.

In 1945, when Mama was almost forty-five,

the primary department superintendent first approached her about teaching children in Sunday school. Mrs. Whatley had never taught and she had not campaigned for the position. However, it seemed like a better choice than the alternative: She was about to be promoted to the "old ladies class" at West End Baptist Church.

The term "behavior management" had not yet been coined, but Mrs. Whatley believed in it anyway. She had rules for her three children at home and she had rules for all her children at church. Mrs. Whatley expected all children to live by her rules. She never thought of them as suggestions. Rather, when Mrs. Whatley made a rule, she considered it a commandment.

Each first Sunday in October, the Southern Baptist New Year, Mrs. Whatley led her new group of children in making their own personal rules. For the next twelve months these simple statements became the behavior management plan that allowed learning to take place between 9:45 and 10:45 A.M. in the Sunday school classroom. For many years I served as the resident "artist," printing these rules on poster paper for Mrs. Whatley. Her grandson Mark assumed the responsibility when, at ten years old, his talent surpassed that of his mother.

Mrs. Whatley's favorite age for a child was six. Six-year-olds were still innocent and eager to learn, and they were old enough to live by the rules. At least most of them were.

And then there was J.J.

I am not sure what the rules were the year J.J. was six, but I am sure he broke every one of them. When J.J. arrived in his new department the first Sunday in October, he had a Bible in one hand, offering envelope in the other, and "challenge" written across his forehead.

Now Mrs. Whatley prided herself that she had never met a child she could not handle. But J.J. was the cumulative of every problem that preceded or ever followed him in Mrs. Whatley's Sunday school class. J.J. talked when he should have listened. He never shared or learned his memory verses. He spoke in a loud voice and did not mind Mrs. Whatley or any of the other teachers. He was unfriendly, unkind, and unruly. J.J. never raised his hand to answer a question in the "big group." In fact, he rarely ever came to group time. While the other children were learning about Abraham, Moses, and Jesus, J.J. stood at the window and looked out or climbed out. He was playing on the porch while the other children were reciting John 3:16.

Mrs. Whatley tried everything. She reminded, pleaded, and encouraged. Between Sunday morning at 10:45 when he left and the following Sunday at 9:45 when he always came back, she fretted and then prayed about what she should do.

She always assigned a teacher to sit beside him. She sometimes turned a chair toward the wall and had him sit in it. This was during the early 1960s so this may have been the original "time-out." Mrs. Whatley was frustrated, but she was never willing to give up on a child. "I have never had a child I couldn't win over," she said. "I will find something he is interested in and then he will settle down."

One Sunday, about six months after J.J. came to disrupt the otherwise orderly class, something remarkable happened. J.J. appeared to be fascinated with Mrs. Whatley; he could not take his eyes off her. He followed her to small group and completed his first-ever Sunday school activity. He learned his Bible verse. Meanwhile, he never took his eyes off his bewildered teacher.

He even went to large group. As teachers and children sat in the large circle, Mrs. Whatley told the Bible story and J.J. leaned forward and watched her every move. Something happened that morning that caught his attention and held it.

Mrs. Whatley was elated. She had finally helped her most difficult child to sit still, pay attention, and follow the rules. Something—she didn't know or care what—had reached this child. She envisioned that J.J. was learning lessons that might change his destiny.

But just before Mrs. Whatley finished the story, J.J. could no longer contain himself. He blurted out, not in his soft voice, "Mrs. Whatley, I've been in your class for a long time and this is the first time you ever got a new dress!"

J.J. is thirty-something now and I hear that he did eventually learn to live by rules. Only eternity can measure the impact those simple words printed on poster paper had on J.J. and hundreds of other precious, impressionable, six-year-old minds.

When Mrs. Whatley's grandson grew up, got married, and went on to seminary, she made her own posters as she had in the early years.

At almost ninety she was still teaching the children, still making rules and posters. Her last poster hung on the wall for months after her death, until her "girls" who had taught with her for many years finally took it down. Moses might have destroyed the tablet of the original commandments, but Mrs. Whatley's commandments were carefully stored in a closet at her church. They were returned to me years later.

OUR RULES

- LISTEN WHILE OTHERS TALK
- SHARE WITH OTHERS
- LEARN OUR MEMORY VERSE
- OBEY OUR TEACHERS
- SPEAK WITH A QUIET VOICE
- WALK IN THE HALLS
- RAISE YOUR HAND IN LARGE GROUPS
- HELP CLEAN UP YOUR TABLE
- BE FRIENDLY
- BE KIND

This past weekend her other grandson was home for a family funeral, and the two of us took a look at Mrs. Whatley's last binding agreement between teacher and child. The poster paper has yellowed with time, but the words, printed in Mrs. Whatley's amazingly steady hand, remain relevant.

Alan and I decided that the world would be a better place if everyone listened. . .shared. . .obeyed those in charge. . .spoke in quiet voices. . .walked instead of ran. . .took turns. . .cleaned up their messes. . .and were kind and friendly.

NEEDLEWORK

I have begun an heirloom-quality project. My target date for completion is Christmas, not this year, but one year later, if all goes well. It will be a gift for Ethan, my only grandson.

The cross-stitch project depicts a small boy dressed in Victorian clothing. A train encircles his feet, as well as a football, building blocks, and a winsome teddy bear. The child is engrossed in the toy he holds, a biplane.

Mama, who died almost three years before

Ethan was born, didn't live long enough to cross-stitch an heirloom for him. So while this won't be "handmade by Mama" quality, I will do my best. As I stitch, I find myself thinking of the handmade heirlooms Mama left to me.

In 1926, while Mama's sister Naomi awaited the birth of her first child, Mama was busy creating an embroidered masterpiece. As was the custom of that time, she used a stamped design.

"We used to buy everything in a kit," Mama explained to me more than once. "The kit would have the fabric with a design stamped on it. It had directions, thread, and anything else you needed to make the piece. It even had a needle in it! The only thing you needed was a pair of embroidery scissors."

Mama never understood that one other important component was necessary to complete the project: talent!

For her sister's expected child, Mama chose a picture of children and rabbits stamped on linen.

Much of the picture was printed in color. Colored yarn to make the hair and cotton to make the rabbit's tail were also included in the kit. The picture was Mama's gift to her niece, Doris Elaine, the first grandchild born to Lillie and George, and it hung in Elaine's room until she was a big girl and decided it was a "baby" picture.

By this time Mama was married and having babies of her own. Since the picture was not being used, and Mama's handwork time was nonexistent, Naomi brought the picture to our house for Mama to hang for her children. Many years later, when the youngest one of us also declared it a "baby" picture, the framed treasure was sentenced to live in Mama's attic. The picture was gone but hardly forgotten.

Mama brought the picture to my house shortly after the birth of my first child. "You probably don't want this old picture, but you can have it if you want," she offered. It was then that she explained to me the history of this yellowed piece of framed fabric. The walls of the nursery were bare, so I hung it over the baby bed of my first son and later the children that followed. Inevitably, the day came when my boys announced they did not want the picture anymore, and again the family heirloom was stored in yet another attic, where it lived for ten years or more.

I happened upon the picture one Saturday afternoon when I was looking for something far less important. After dusting if off, I saw for the first time the love and talent displayed in every stitch. And to think this prized possession had spent more than fifty years in an attic! Finally, I was old enough to recognize a treasure.

But the picture needed refurbishing, and I trusted only one business in our city to do the job. Without telling Mama I had found the picture, I called Chilton's Art and Framing. Beautifully restored and reframed weeks later (it cost about the same amount of money I spent each month to feed my family), I hung it with pride in the master bedroom.

The month was November and our extended family, including cousin Elaine, celebrated Thanksgiving at my house. I took her into my bedroom and told her that I wanted her to see my new picture. As she admired the exquisite handwork, she gazed more closely at the children holding rabbits. She had a puzzled look on her face.

"That's my picture!" she said.

"No, it's my picture!" I replied. I reminded her that she had not wanted the picture anymore because it was a "baby" picture. Even today we joke about the ownership of the picture. Two houses later, it still hangs in my bedroom.

Mama was delighted when I found the picture and thought it worthy of hanging in what she called my "nice house." One day I made the mistake of telling her what I spent to have it restored. She said, "You could've bought a big nice framed print for your wall with all that money!" She never could accept that any of her exquisite handwork was anything special.

"I can still do that embroidering," Mama volunteered on one of the many Thursday nights we stood admiring the picture. "I've been practicing on some handkerchiefs. I still have some iron-on transfers from the thirties." She was referring to the 1930s, a half-century ago!

The year was 1981, and Don and I were about to celebrate our twenty-fifth wedding anniversary. I thought Mama would ask me what I wanted her to buy for us for an anniversary gift. I knew what I wanted—something handmade, something embroidered.

But without any prior requests from me, she came to visit one Thursday with a little package in a Gayfer's bag. She had found and purchased a twenty-fifth anniversary kit, stamped fabric, directions, and thread included. "This kit even has a hoop in it," she said. "But I don't use a hoop. It just gets in my way." When she was trying to do something, Mama never liked for anything or anyone to get in her way.

Mama enjoyed the handwork after busying her hands with more strenuous tasks for many years. "This piece is coming right along," Mama would say each week as she displayed it for me. "It should be ready by December."

"I'm having trouble with the birds," Mama announced one week. She always fought with the birds that ate her figs and blueberries, but this was fall, so I could not imagine what she was talking about. Her reply was, "Not those birds, the love-birds! You know!" Actually, I didn't know, but she was anxious to show me.

At the lower edge of the anniversary sampler were two perfectly embroidered lovebirds encircled by an elaborate display of ribbon and flowers. "You see," she said, "this is the second time I have done these. I had them finished and I didn't like the way they looked. So I ripped them out. And now they don't look a bit better. I wanted them to be perfect!"

They looked perfect to me, but she proceeded to

pluck every "feather" off with her scissors. She made a third set with new thread. "This is better," she said several weeks later. "It's not as good as I wanted it to be, but I guess it will have to do." I wanted to tell her that it is difficult to improve on perfection.

At the party we gave to celebrate our anniversary, we displayed the beautiful sampler by the cake. Everyone who came admired it. Naturally, Mama was nearby enjoying their comments and pointing out the imperfections that only she could see. She mentioned the lovebirds to everyone. Even the third set of feathers still did not meet her high standard.

Sometimes as I pass through the study off my bedroom I stop and spend a few minutes with those birds. It still escapes me how she could have felt anything but pride when she completed them. But Mama was a perfectionist and nothing she ever made was perfect enough. The older I get, the more I look and act like her. And now I understand why she wanted to do her best.

In a hotel room in Philadelphia, Pennsylvania, I spent several hours cross-stitching a wing on the little boy's toy plane. It wasn't perfect, so I spent hours ripping it out and redoing it. I wanted it to be perfect because I love the little boy—not the little boy in the picture, but the one who will get the picture for Christmas some year.

Finally, I understand the lovebirds. When Mama gave to those she loved, she wanted to give only her best, as nearly perfect as she could make it. And I want to do the same.

WEDDING DRESS

Later in her life, Mama's mother, Lillie, supplemented her income by making wedding attire for that segment of society that is still referred to as "Old Mobile." Affluent families often used a local seamstress to create the wedding gown, the bridesmaids' dresses, and the wedding attire for the mothers of the bride and groom. Sometimes Lillie was asked to create the "going away" outfit and other honeymoon finery.

Mama, who inherited Lillie's sewing genes,

made articles of clothing for others, but never received money for her sewing. For Mama, sewing was an act of love. As her daughter, I was a lifelong recipient of those homemade acts of love. But for some reason I cannot explain, I bought my wedding dress.

Mama's wedding dress creation was further delayed when my only daughter, her only grand-daughter, died in infancy. So it fell to Mama's great-granddaughter, Jessica, to be the fortunate recipient of the only wedding dress Mama ever made.

The dress has been stored for many years, but recently I asked Karen, Jessica's mother, to unpack the dress for us to enjoy again. I examined the tiny stitches, handmade trim, lined bodice, and perfectly gathered skirt. Holding the dress brought back vivid memories of the beautiful ceremony and how special Jessica was and still is today.

Mama had not planned to make the wedding dress. It just happened.

Don and I were visiting on St. Simon's Island with a friend, Eileen, who was making a wedding dress for her niece out of a beautiful white eyelet. After returning home, yards of the beautiful fabric I had admired arrived at our home—a gift from Eileen! And the rest, as they say, is history.

Mama was a little nervous about making the dress, but the rest of the family was confident. She measured Jessica's petite body. She chose a pattern and then she began the lengthy process of making her first wedding dress. She was eighty-five years old at the time. As was her nature, she planned ahead that she would worry until the dress was completed.

Mama often said, "The most important part of making a dress is to cut it properly." She never needed her scissors on the first day of dress construction; she only needed fabric and pattern. The first day was for "placing the fabric," Mama said.

This dress pattern had to be placed perfectly to insure that the bodice and sleeves could be cut from the embossed area of the fabric and still leave ample scalloped lace edging for the ankle-length dress. Mama placed and replaced the pattern, taking into consideration the right and wrong side of the fabric and the fact that only one edge was scalloped. She was finally ready to cut.

The day she actually cut out the wedding dress I received a call at work from my secretary that I should call my mother immediately. Mama was sobbing when she answered the telephone. She had cut the bodice wrong. She was certain Jessica would not be wearing that dress on the wedding day.

After the tears subsided, I assured her the dress was not important enough that it should make her have a second heart attack. We would work something out, and if we couldn't, I would buy more fabric. Mama, who knew no more fabric was available, continued to worry. But eventually she was consoled enough to work out what was eventually no problem at all.

She finished the cutting and started the basting. She had to work from measurements because Jessica lived five hundred miles away. Of course, when Jessica tried the dress on for the first time after it was completely finished, no one was surprised that it fit perfectly!

I have the heirloom dress hanging beside me as I write. The bodice has a high empire waist and a plain round neck. The short capped sleeves are softly gathered at each shoulder and the lower edge of the sleeves is scalloped. The long skirt is gathered and drops from the empire yoke. The delicate eyelet design at the top of the skirt becomes more pronounced as it forms deep scallops at the lower ankle-length edge. The handmade tatting, which encircles the neck and scalloped edges of the capped sleeves, completes the dress. Clearly, it's an act of love made by Mama for her only great-granddaughter.

Today is Jessica's birthday. She is thirteen years old. The wedding was ten years ago, just before her third birthday. She slept through the ceremony in the arms of her great-uncle, while her aunt Debbi walked down the aisle in an exquisite white gown to marry Jessica's uncle Mark, our younger son.

The wedding album tells the story of the day. Shots taken from the balcony of the church record candles, flowers, and a wedding party of twenty-four. And a candid shot at the reception reveals a happy great-grandmother, Mama, chatting with friends.

Like the members of the bridal party, Jessica posed for her formal portrait prior to the ceremony. But my favorite picture of her in the wedding dress was taken at the reception, after she had finished her nap. She is in her papa's arms, and he is also holding Jessica's doll that is clothed in a dress identical to Jessica's. It even has handmade tatting at the neck. Jessica is wearing a gold bracelet and pearls like those worn by the wedding attendants. Her hair is pulled back and held in place by a lace and ribbon barrette. She is wearing a corsage with mauve ribbon, one of the wedding colors.

She was not quite three years old, but she was almost as radiant as the bride, and no wonder. She was wearing her own beautiful heirloom wedding dress, handmade by Mama.

TRIPS

In the high country of Wyoming, home of the Grand Tetons, a one-hour hike along Jackson Lake offers a spectacular view. When I visited in mid-September, the foliage was turning and the mountains were snowcapped. How I wish I could tell Mama about my hike in the Tetons!

Mama loved to travel.

She often told the story of the first trip she took soon after the Sciple family moved from the country to the small town of DeKalb, Mississippi. Her father, George, worked at the cotton mill, had the Aladdin Lamp franchise, was Justice of the Peace, and taught a Sunday school class at the Methodist Church. George had developed a friendship with his minister, and the two men took their families on a camping trip to an area near Sciple's Mill.

The families traveled by horse and wagon on what was only a trail at the time. (Today it is known as Mississippi State Road 39.) Happy children anticipated playing together, frying fish and eating outside, and eating desserts prepared at home. The families bedded down on quilts in the schoolhouse, deserted for the summer vacation. A fierce summer thunderstorm at midnight frightened the children and probably the adults, too.

When Mama was past eighty, she was still returning to the area of her birth to visit. She and her sisters loved to point out the exact spot they had camped seventy years earlier. "That is where the schoolhouse was, and Mr. Sam Creekmore lived at the bottom of the hill!" "Yes!" the others chimed in. But they never could agree if "Mr. Sam" lived on the right or the left. Mama's ninety-four-year-old sister recently said to me, "I'm sure it was on the right!" She is probably correct, since Mama also always voted for the right.

When the family moved farther south to Mobile and Mama joined the downtown working girls, she met a young woman named Claudia. The two developed a lifelong friendship. Claudia married "Cook" (actually his last name) from Steubenville, Ohio.

In the 1920s Ohio was a foreign country to Mama. In fact, Ohio was probably little known to many in the South, as these were the early days of "distant" travel by automobile. But Claudia and Cook decided to travel to Ohio and invited Mama to accompany them. The three left in Cook's old Ford before the roads were paved or the KOA's were built.

When night came, the three set up camp, cooked outside, and then bedded down for the night. This was repeated at least three nights, and sometimes more, when it rained and travel became difficult. When his car got stuck on the muddy roads, Cook just waited until another car approached, and then the men pushed his car, by hand, to firmer ground.

Mama was the sole support of her family, and her parents did not approve of her dating, for obvious reasons. But on each trip to Steubenville she was introduced to a new beau, and her old picture album displays Mama posing cozily with more than one of them.

From her early travel adventures, Mama learned the world was larger than Mobile, Alabama. Perhaps her interest in travel stemmed from the beautiful maps she drew at school.

Mama traveled by train to Atlanta, Georgia, and then West Palm Beach, Florida, to visit a married sister. She returned to West Palm Beach when her current Mobile beau (and future husband), Henry, was working there. Henry remained her beau from

1925 until 1931, when they finally married. Mama often implied that Daddy wanted to get married much sooner. Eventually, he was so fed up with her family responsibilities interfering with her freedom that he just told her they were getting married. After all, she was thirty-one years old!

Fortunately, Mama married a man who also loved to travel. In fact, he went on a trip nearly every week. His favorite, and only, destination, however, was the place of his birth, thirty miles north of Mobile and three miles southwest of Citronelle on Sand Ridge Road.

"Get your bath and get in bed early tonight," Mama told us almost every Friday night. "We're going to the country tomorrow." All of us children loved those words! We would play with the country cousins, drink cool water from a dipper on the back porch, and hope for rain on the tin roof. If we stayed late enough, we could enjoy the lighting of lanterns. This mystical light was much more exciting to us than that produced by the flip of a switch at home!

Mama's "distant" travel was curtailed for many years. But after Daddy's death, travel became an important part of Mama's survival plan. She made numerous trips to the place of her birth in Mississippi to fish in the ponds at Sciple's Mill, and she traveled with her sisters and my family. But her best travel days were yet to come.

Something happened during the seventies in America that was perfect timing for Mama. Senior citizen travel groups were formed, made up mostly of blue-haired ladies and a few balding men. They packed their polyester pantsuits, chartered buses, and hit the newly built interstates en masse. Mama and another lifelong friend and traveling buddy, Irene, joined the Gulf Coast senior citizens, and Mama became a transient. She went on day trips, week-long trips, and almost month-long trips. Every trip was her favorite, and each one was more fun than the last, until she went to Wyoming.

Before her first trip to the Tetons (and before any excursion she considered), Mama fretted over the travel expenses. She discussed the trip with herself, her son, her daughter, and her son-in-law, in that order. First, she convinced herself the trip was too expensive. While her son and daughter could not change her mind, however, her son-in-law could always convince her to go. "I think you should stay home and save all that money," Don would tease. "You need to leave it all to me so I can spend it when you're gone!"

"Don, you know you don't mean that!" was Mama's standard retort. But he gave her just enough impetus to insure she would be on the bus when it left Mobile.

Those busloads of blue-haired little ladies and their few balding men went from the Greek Church in Malbis near Mobile to Maine to see the brilliant foliage of fall. They traveled from DisneyWorld to Fisherman's Wharf in San Francisco. Mama and

Irene were with them when they went to the state capital in Montgomery for an overnight visit and when they went to Calgary and the Columbia ice fields. A favorite excursion of Mama's was Victoria, British Columbia, and Butchart Gardens.

This strict Southern Baptist lady even went to Las Vegas and frequented the casinos until the early morning hours. She told us later with a little giggle, "You know I didn't gamble!" But she was always afraid her preacher would hear she had gone to "that sinful place."

Still, there was one trip that stood taller than any other in Mama's mind. She made the same trip three times and loved each one more than the one before. Her favorite place on the face of this earth was the Grand Tetons.

Her first trip there brought a deluge of postcards to my mailbox that included pictures of Jackson Hole, Jackson Lake Lodge, and the Grand Tetons. When I met the bus, she gushed, "You and Don have got to go there!" She had made a master plan for her daughter's travel.

She patiently showed me even more postcards and tried with not so gentle persuasion to convince us to plan a trip to Jackson Hole. Rather than Jackson Hole, we went to Hawaii. She was patient, but when we bypassed the Tetons to go on a Caribbean cruise, she was a little more than exasperated. And she surely never understood when we crossed the Atlantic on a plane to go to Europe!

Finally, after she died, Don and I spent six days in Jackson Hole, Wyoming. We walked the streets of the town she loved. We went to Jenny Lake Lodge and enjoyed the gourmet buffet in the dining room. We ate the same chuck wagon dinner that she raved about, and then we watched the same entertainment at the Bar J Ranch. We even stayed at her beloved Jackson Lake Lodge. Of all the places she ever hung her hat, I think this was her favorite.

Now I think I understand. This may be the most

beautiful place on earth, at least the part of the earth that Mama visited. Mama always wanted whatever was best and most beautiful for me. She didn't have to say it with words. All she had to do was push me in the right direction.

She would have been happy to know I finally did what she told me to do. I went to the Tetons! And when I was there, I had a feeling that she did know.

TATTING

Recently I explored the attic, the place where Mama's life is stored in boxes. I was looking for something insignificant, but instead I found a treasure.

Gingerly, I stroked the circular piece of fabric, about sixteen inches in diameter. It is hemmed with almost perfect tiny stitches. The fabric is a fine grade of cotton or perhaps linen. This table doily is encircled by a two-inch-wide border of what we used to call "poor man's lace" or tatting. It was handmade by my mother, I am sure. The minute stitches I see in the hemmed edge are her trademark. Yellowed by many years of storage and stained in three places, it is my treasure.

Tatting, a unique knitting process, was developed about the turn of this century, just about the time Mama was born. Although the lace looks fragile and dainty, it is quite strong and it lasts for years—some say long enough to be passed down for many generations. This was not the first sample of Mama's tatting I had ever seen.

When Mama turned eighty-six years old, Don and I built our dream home. I was determined every item I purchased would be special and chosen with love and care.

Mama and I shopped together for hand towels for the powder room. She looked for bargains as I admired the exquisite linen covered with lace. My frugal mother told me quickly I did not need to spend so much money on those little towels to "put in a bathroom!" And then she said, "If you want some towels with tatting on them, just buy some linen towels and I will make the tatting."

I raised my eyebrows. "You can make that lace?" I was astonished! She didn't even know how to crochet.

"Indeed I can," she answered, "so you don't have to waste your money buying towels with 'machine tatting' on them. I'll just have to find my shuttle."

Mama found her shuttle and I bought some good cotton thread. She refreshed the memory of her fingers as she practiced for the job at hand, making tatting for the plain linen towels.

Her first efforts frustrated her; I was afraid she'd probably forgotten the art over her many years. But Mama would say as she practiced, "Tatting is like riding a wheel." ("Wheel" was the word Mama always used for bicycle.) And then she'd add, "Once you learn to do it, you can always do it. You just have to practice a little."

To my amazement, Mama quickly remastered

the art. One Thursday evening when she arrived for her visit she brought a sample for my inspection and approval. I gazed at the intricate stitching. "It looks perfect to me!" I cried delightedly. Only then was she willing to start on the fourteen-inch strips for the towels.

As we visited after supper on another Thursday night soon after the towels were finished, Mama posed her usual fall question: "What do you want me to buy you for Christmas this year?" Although always careful with her money, each year she wanted to buy a special Christmas present for me.

Without hesitating, I told her I wanted more tatting. "That is not a good Christmas present," Mama said. "I will make all the tatting you want, but I need to know what you want for Christmas." After much persuasion, she agreed to make a doily, but she was still unconvinced of its merit as a Christmas gift.

When I opened my package from Mama on Christmas Eve, my eyes beheld a treasure. The intricate doily consisted of a tatted center, surrounded by six identical circles that formed an exquisite piece of handwork. She had even taken it to the frame shop to have it matted and framed.

I found the perfect place for the tatting to live—in my dressing room, next to my sink. This special place gave me the opportunity to see it and enjoy it many times each day.

Still Mama was not satisfied. It bothered her that I did not have a special present, which to her meant a store-bought one. So she spent some of her limited money to buy me a surprise. Funny, today I can't even recall what the store-bought present was, but the framed tatting continues to bring me joy.

As soon as the Christmas decorations were packed away each year, Mama began to fret about what to give the grandsons and their wives for their birthdays. It did not matter that their birthdays were not until July and October. She seemed to need something to worry about, and birthday presents made a perfect worry for cold January days.

When I suggested she give them gifts of homemade tatting, she was not sure. "Barbara," she said, "you may appreciate those little lace doilies, but your children won't think they are real presents." But I was persistent and Mama finally relented. Of course, everyone loved the birthday presents. But Mama truly never understood.

When fall came again I was prepared for the Christmas question. My answer was all ready: "I want more tatting!"

"You want more tatting?" Mama asked. "I wish you would let me buy something special for you this year."

I knew Mama was approaching the end. Those busy fingers would soon get their much-deserved rest. I realized with growing poignancy that everything she made with those wrinkled hands would be special, very special. I could only imagine what the tiny pieces of handmade love would mean to all of us later.

Mama proceeded to buy a set of ivory sheets with pillowcases to match (on sale, of course). This year's Christmas tatting would be long narrow strips of the intricate handwork, identical to the original fourteen-inch pieces attached to the hand towels. She sewed these durable yet dainty pieces of lace to the edges of the pillowcases and wrapped them with the sheets for my Christmas present. (And, of course, she included the obligatory store-bought present.)

Christmas afternoon, Mama left on an afternoon flight, going home with one grandson and his wife to spend a week in Texas. I knew she had packed her mother-of-pearl tatting shuttle, the original one, which dated back to the early 1900s. Mark and Debbi had asked their Mamaw to teach them to tat.

Some say tatting is easy, but Mark and Debbi didn't think so. Karen, Mama's other granddaughter-in-love, didn't think so either when she later bought a shuttle and tried to master the art. They never learned to tat, but they did make beautiful memories with their Mamaw.

I watched Mama work with her shuttle and thread for endless hours. I'm sorry I never asked her to teach me. Some say tatting is a dying art. Sadly, for our family it proved to be true. But after she brought in a new decade in Texas with the grand-children who didn't quite learn to tat, Mama returned home with a mission. "I am going to make tatting for all of them for Christmas!" She added, "I'm going to buy the sheets and pillowcases during the January white sale. I'll make a set for each fam-ily." And she did.

Every Thursday she brought the shuttle and thread to my house, spending hours working on those long strips of lace. Each strip had to be per-fect. As usual, anything that Mama did had no room for imperfection.

Mama and I wrapped those presents on

December 12, 1990. Earlier that day she had helped to decorate the Christmas tree in my living room. One set of sheets was placed under the tree. The other set was mailed to Mark and Debbi, who would be spending their first Christmas away from home.

Two days later Mama's hands folded in death.

Christmas Day the grandchildren experienced a bittersweet moment as they opened their last tangible gift from Mamaw. Some may still say tatting is "poor man's lace." But Mama's grandchildren know tatting is a piece of handmade love, and they feel rich indeed.

MUSIC

Mama never played a musical instrument or sang a solo. She never even sang in a choir. But music was an important part of her life. It may have even been the reason her parents met and married.

In the mid-1880s, Mama's grandfather, Alonzo Vandevender, was the proprietor of the hotel-boardinghouse in Shuqualak, Mississippi. Alonzo and his wife, Margaret Elizabeth ("Megarah"), had four daughters, but it was the youngest one, Lillie, who played the piano for the guests in the boardinghouse dining room. Lillie may have had some lessons, but Mama always said she "played by ear."

The tiny town of Shuqualak, pronounced "shug-a-lock," was the first stop north of Meridian on the Mobile and Ohio railroad line. When Mama's father, George, who had been offered a college education by a wealthy New York relative, began his trip north, he stayed overnight at the Shuqualak Hotel so he could catch the early train.

There George met Lillie as she entertained in the dining room. They married at the turn of the century and headed east by train to Atlanta, Georgia, on their honeymoon. I have a lovely portrait of the couple dressed in their wedding attire. George is seated and Lillie is standing, as was the custom of that time.

George and Lillie "set up housekeeping" and started a family. They bought a piano, and Lillie continued to play. She sometimes even played for weddings.

Many years later, when I was a child, I heard Lillie play. I have a faint memory of her playing and singing "When They Ring Those Golden Bells for You and Me." The music was pretty, but I remember feeling sad.

Mama had some piano lessons, but she never really learned to play. At least, that's what she would tell me. (As an adult I took three years of expensive piano lessons and I really never learned to play. I can find middle C, but only if the piano is a Baldwin.) Still, Mama was blessed with some musical talent.

When Mama was in the kitchen, where she spent much of my childhood, she was singing. Her voice would not have won a vocal contest, but it sounded beautiful to me. If Mama were singing, she was happy. And at our house, everybody wanted Mama to be happy.

She sang the old church hymns: "Near the Cross," "Sweet Hour of Prayer," and another favorite, "Trust and Obey." In her lifetime she did a lot of trusting and plenty of obeying. And anytime Mama sang, she concluded her concert with "What a Friend We Have in Jesus." She only knew one verse from memory, so she just sang it over and over.

When my father died suddenly, an acquaintance named Betts offered to sing at the funeral. She asked me what we wanted her to sing. Twenty-three years old, less than twenty-four hours after the death of my father, I didn't have an answer.

The next day as the service began, Betts stood and sang the song she had chosen. It was Mama's special song.

What a friend we have in Jesus
All our sins and griefs to bear!
What a privilege to carry
Everything to God in prayer!
Oh, what peace we often forfeit
Oh, what needless pain we bear
All because we do not carry
Everything to Him in prayer.

While watching the Billy Graham crusades on television, Mama heard George Beverly Shea and promptly added "How Great Thou Art" to her repertoire of favorite songs.

For forty-five years Mama also sang to the children she taught in Sunday school. But the height of her vocal career was when she sang to her grandchildren. The two grandsons often went to Mama's house to spend the night, and Mama loved to rock them in the old platform rocker in her living room, singing all the while. I would ask the boys when they returned home if their Mamaw rocked them. I couldn't remember her rocking and singing to me, and I wanted my own children to remember this special time with her. She rocked and sang to them until their feet dragged on the floor!

Years later, her turn came to sit for hours and listen to each of her grandsons perform for her on Thursday night. One played the piano and the other the piano and the guitar. She always asked Mark to play "How Great Thou Art." When she would sometimes doze off, they weren't quite sure if they should continue, but they knew she loved their music. So they just kept on playing.

She loved most of their music, but she did not like rock music. Mama was much more excited about Alan playing "Why Me, Lord" on his guitar than she was about him going to a rock concert. Those were the early days of rock and drugs. Mama would tell him, "Alan, I'm afraid if you go to that rock concert, someone will slip up behind you when you aren't looking and shoot you with that marijuana!"

In her last years Mama sat in the same pew each Sunday morning with the same two special friends. Alan always affectionately said they sang off-key in "old lady squeaky kind of voices."

Near the end, though, Mama didn't sing, even in church. She just stood and held her hymnal, opened to the right page. She said she just didn't have the breath to sing anymore.

Before Mark left for seminary, he gave one last piano concert at a local church he served while in college. Mama was sitting there as proud as any grandparent could be. To close the concert Mark said, "I want to dedicate this song to my grandmother, who is here tonight. This is her favorite song." And then he did his beautiful rendition of "How Great Thou Art."

Several years passed before Mark played Mama's song again. This time it was in her church. I read my tribute to Mama, and Alan read the poem he had written two weeks earlier.

A TRIBUTE TO MAMA

Mama died Friday December 14, 1990, at the age of eighty-nine, almost ninety. Mama received little formal education in her day, but she was an honor graduate in the school of hard work, an expert in the language of vegetable gardens and little children.

She never wrote a book, composed a poem, or painted a masterpiece. She never sang a solo or made a public speech, and she led few public prayers. Her name only appeared in the newspaper once before her obituary column was published. Hers was a life of deeds rather than words.

Mama did not leave a lot of material wealth. But to those who knew her, she left a legacy of loving service and simple living. Her personal wants were few, but she wanted the best for others.

Mama's great loves were her family, her vegetable garden, and a deep and unusual love for the little children she taught for over forty years.

I know she earned a crown for her quiet services, for the Scriptures say, "Inasmuch as ye have done it unto one of the least of these. . .ye have done it unto me."

In the words of Solomon, "I will arise and call her blessed."

Barbara Sims,
December 17, 1990

TO MAMAW'S HOUSE
(to say good-bye)

An ancient fading dress
held your spirit then.
I held you, a thin stone tower
smiling through pale eyes and wrinkles.
You would be gone soon, you said,
sharing bread with Jesus, seeing "Daddy" again.
When I was small and you said that
I waited for you to leave,
knowing that you never lied,
only to relax in the end
thinking you were mistaken.

We talked about Bud and Billy
and the family Bible with the birthdays in it.
Darkness pressed us from all directions
because light costs money
and shows too much anyway.

We turned the lights on once,
and having photographed another moment,
returned quickly to your comfortable shadow.

I showed your great-grandchild the places
that started my memories of you.
I showed her the pond where we fished
and told her stories of whales and serpents,
hoping she would remember your face.
In the end I wondered
if I should have been there at all,
eating your gumbo one last time,
watching you fetch the final shrimp
from the bottom of your bottomless pot.

ALAN SIMS,
November 30, 1990

Then Mark left the pew where we sat as a family, crossed the front of her church, sat down at the piano, and played from memory her song. He had never played that wonderful hymn more beautifully. His eyes, and ours, were filled with tears. This was Mama's memorial service.

Everyone's eyes were filled with tears when at the conclusion of the service our dear friend, Paul Hancock, stood and sang these words:

O Lord, my God!
When I in awesome wonder
Consider all the worlds
Thy hands have made
I see the stars,
I hear the rolling thunder,
Thy power throughout
the universe displayed.
When Christ shall come
with shouts of acclamation.

And take me home,
what joy shall fill my heart!
Then I shall bow
in humble adoration,
And then proclaim, my God,
how great Thou art!

The entire congregation then rose to their feet
and joined in singing.

THEN SINGS MY SOUL,
MY SAVIOR GOD, TO THEE;
HOW GREAT THOU ART,
HOW GREAT THOU ART!
THEN SINGS MY SOUL,
MY SAVIOR GOD, TO THEE;
HOW GREAT THOU ART,
HOW GREAT THOU ART!

Mama's life song was over. In heaven she has a

new voice; she doesn't have to use the squeaky old lady one anymore. She's somewhere up there singing her favorites. . .maybe even in the choir. . . and maybe even accompanied by Lillie (by ear, of course).

LEGACY

I turn off the asphalt of Celeste Road onto the dirt of Lambert Cemetery Road. The ever-present ruts in the sandy surface intimidate me, so I put my car tires where they tell me. I proceed slowly and carefully toward the destination that draws me. As usual, I cannot do otherwise.

Almost five years have gone by since I read my tribute, Alan read his poem, and Mark played Mama's favorite song. Still, whenever I travel this route, I feel a compelling urge to spend a few minutes at the gravesite of my mother. I find myself following the ruts and pulling up the washed clay incline to park next to the long abandoned church.

The story goes that Daddy's sister, Aunt Nora, had a religious experience as an adult and started preaching. Daddy built the little wooden building as a place for her to hold her Pentecostal-type services. As young children we simply called it "Aunt Nora's church." When her health failed and she could no longer preach, the building remained vacant, and over time it deteriorated.

I always feel a little uncomfortable when I park beside the church on my frequent trips. Nevertheless, I do the inevitable. I get out of the car, lock the door, walk past the small rectangular building without a steeple, and open the double-width gate that leads to the fenced cemetery.

City cemeteries often have acres of treeless expanse and matching markers for each gravesite. Those who control the business decide what kind of flowers may be placed to honor the dead and how soon they must be removed. Individuals are hired to mow the lawn and weed near the granite slabs that cover the gravesites.

But Lambert Cemetery is different. This country cemetery is a rectangular expanse of lawn with a simple defining fence. Cedar trees from yesteryear are sprinkled among the tombstones. Some tombstones were made by hand with names etched by family members while the mortar was still soft. Newer commercial markers stand more erect and display perfectly imprinted names. All except the very newest headstones show varying signs of weathering stain. Wildflowers, baskets of plastic flowers, dying wreaths from a recent funeral, and even a pile of discarded flowers give recognition and respect to those buried here. Living family members tidy up the area of their own "family plot."

My first experience with the strong sting of death was one Friday in May. I was twenty-three years old and too young to bury my father. A few short months later, a much smaller casket was placed in the ground on a cold January morning. Today a headstone with an angel watches over the burial place of our only daughter, Joy.

But the space between those two is what brings me here now. I sometimes sit on the grass, or if the grass is damp, on the granite slab that covers Mama's grave. And I think.

At first I couldn't think; I just sat and cried all the tears that would not come during her last weeks of illness and the days immediately following her death. I had wanted to be strong, brave for the children and granddaughter, and in control. But by now most of my tears have been shed and I can think.

Sometimes when I think it makes me sad. Mama's only great-grandchild was seven when Mama died, and Jessica's memories are already dim. Mama never had the chance to hold or kiss Ethan, her great-grandson, born years after her death. He never had the opportunity to be rocked by Mama as she sang "Bringing in the Sheaves."

Sometimes I am sad for selfish reasons. I can't dial 866–7264 and ask about a recipe. I can't chat with her on Thursdays and watch her replace the missing buttons on our clothing. I have had fresh turnips only once since her death five years ago. And we have been without homemade pickles for years.

Other times I am sad for what might have been. I wish I had listened more carefully to the stories she loved to tell about her ancestors, her family, and her growing-up years. I wish I had asked more questions. I wish I had been a more appreciative daughter. I wish we had shared a different mother-daughter relationship. And I wish just once she had said "I love you" to her only daughter.

But more often now I feel peace. The passing of years has allowed me to see a bigger picture. And I see that picture most clearly when I am sitting at the cemetery, remembering. I realize in the big book of time that Mama's life is an important chapter.

She lived a long life, eighty-nine years, eleven months, and eight days. Very few have planted more seeds in a garden or more seeds in the hearts of little children. Surely no one made a better piecrust, rocked a grandchild longer, or delivered more home-grown tomatoes to family and friends. She lived life to its fullest. Mama spent every waking moment in meaningful activity. To do less was "wasting time," or "wasting life."

Even without climbing my stairs to look at the quilt she spent a year of her life making for me, I can see how deeply she loved me. Love is unselfish. What she often said of others can be used to describe her: "There's not a selfish bone in her body."

A car rumbles down the dirt road. I am startled as a bird swoops down and perches in a nearby tree. It seems to be watching me, puzzled, perhaps wondering why someone lingers so long today among still and silent friends. But my mind leaves the bird and swiftly returns to the bigger picture. I realize, in a sense, we still have Mama. We have vivid memories of her. We are surrounded by the tangible evidence of her life. We feel her love in our hearts.

Mama left a beautiful legacy.

It is time to leave and I wonder: Does everyone leave a legacy? As I return to my car, I pass Aunt Nora's church. . .our little daughter's grave. . .and the resting place of my beloved father. I unlock the car door and wonder why I locked it in the first place. And then I know. I locked the door because Mama always thought doors should be locked.

Mama taught her wisdom well. It still shapes my life. That is her legacy, a legacy I can pass on to my own children and to their children. I can almost see the heritage of love stretching into the future like a long and indestructible chain.